Praise for *All Dreams on Deck*

"Jeremy Cage has written a great book that everyone who thinks about how to better balance work–life issues would benefit from reading. Everything starts with a dream—but Jeremy really shows us how to get started on making these dreams come to life. Generalities won't get it done; it requires very specific charting and execution. Just as Jeremy navigated his way across oceans, he's also shown us how we can better navigate life's personal and professional challenges. I'm giving my daughters copies of his book, and I hope they get as much out of Jeremy's insights as I did."

—Katie Couric, journalist and author, Yahoo!
Global News anchor

"How I wish *All Dreams on Deck* was available when ISE first launched, but it might even be more valuable now as I near retirement. Jeremy Cage presents a well-developed process for improving the odds of accomplishing your professional and personal goals through the fine art of storytelling, sailing you around the world and teaching you the mentality needed to realize your life-long dreams. When I finished reading, I could smell the ocean. More importantly, I had learned invaluable lessons to help me navigate future endeavors."

—Gary Katz, cofounder, president, and CEO
of International Securities Exchange (ISE)

"Jeremy does a masterful job of taking us with him on his journey as he weaves lessons for life and work with his adventure of sailing around the world. A very enjoyable and inspirational read. Jeremy urges us to be intentional about our dreams and gives the reader a practical how-to guide."

—Carlos Barroso, senior vice president of research, development,
and quality for the Campbell's Soup Company

"*All Dreams On Deck* is a must read and should be shared with any business team or philanthropic project team you work with. The power in these principles are contagious and will deliver significantly better results and working relationships if followed. This book is so spot-on that I am asking each of my children to read it and to chart an intentional course in life towards their dreams. What an inspiration, Jeremy. Thank you!"

—Kevin Hall, principal and founder of The Brand Charge,
former CEO of the Geneva Watch Group

"*All Dreams on Deck* is an inspiring, practical, and enjoyable guide to making work and personal dreams come true. Jeremy includes wonderful stories about his experience as a CEO, a leader of multibillion-dollar businesses, an entrepreneur, and a dreamer. He's even sailed around the world in a small boat. Grab this delightful book and let Jeremy Cage show you how to begin dreaming again and start realizing those dreams."

—Lisa Hillenbrand, former director of Global Marketing for Procter &
Gamble, coauthor of *Stragility: Excelling at Strategic Changes*

"This book reinforces the importance of having dreams and a well-thought-out plan to achieve them. Jeremy uses examples from his own personal journey to lay out clear and simple steps for moving from aspiration to reality. After reading this book, I'm motivated to make a few of my own long-standing dreams come to life."

—Mark Schiller, president of Pinnacle Foods, Inc.

"If you have dreams, this book helps you turn them into reality. Jeremy gives you some simple frameworks that help you become much more intentional and specific about your dreams, plans, and preparation and then inspires you to be courageous enough to pursue them. A great, easy read for anyone looking to make their dreams come true or change direction and achieve more balance in their lives."

—Melanie Healey, former group president at
Procter & Gamble North America

All

DREAMS

On

DECK

"Jeremy Cage's *All Dreams on Deck* is the perfect compendium of factors to success. Whether it be personal success, business success, or the delicate balance beam of both, his prescriptive insights intertwined with real business vignettes is a terrific recipe for self-realization. I recommend it to anyone wanting to succeed in life!"

—John Dovich, president and CEO of Dovich &
Associates Certified Financial Services

"In a fast-paced world, where many are running too fast, *All Dreams on Deck*, provides a thoughtful reminder to follow our internal compass, charting a course to achieve one's life's passion, purpose, and dharma, which will lead to brighter horizons and a more fulfilling life. *ADOD* is a quick, provocative read, whose simple tools provide a powerful structure and a process for achieving your dreams. Well done!"

—Robert P. Baird Jr, president and CEO of AT Cross

"Most of us are waiting idly for our dreams to come true. Jeremy Cage knows that our best hopes and aspirations must be named out loud, shared with others, and carefully nurtured. Otherwise, our dreams die. If you've forgotten the dreams you used to have, open this book. With Jeremy as a wise and patient guide for this journey, you will soon discover you have sailed into a realm where dreams are no longer just dreams."

—**David Anderson**, rector and author of *Breakfast Epiphanies* and *Losing Your Faith, Finding Your Soul*

"*All Dreams on Deck* was a thoroughly enjoyable read (even for someone with a short attention span) that presents a great foundation and framework for your business dreams and your life dreams."

—**Eric Rowland**, principal and chief architect for Rowland Design

"Inspiring! I love what Jeremy has done. He provides specific tools that we can apply in real time to better our businesses, our own lives, and follow our dreams. I couldn't put the book down once I started reading it; it spoke to me in so many ways."

—**David Veckerelli,** CEO of City Explorer TV

"*All Dreams on Deck* delivers an excellent framework that forces you to ask yourself important questions about your values and aspirations and provides a highly practical blueprint for how you set about making choices that enable you to realize both your personal and professional aspirations."

—**Rick Rizzo**, CEO of Fleet Laboratories

"Jeremy offers a holistic approach to determining, integrating, and enriching your life's priorities. Declaring the mighty power of dreaming big, he not only helps you build the frame of your lifeboat; he inspires you to tap into your least exercised personal capability—courage."

—**Arthur Brown**, head of North America CPG and New York Office for Spencer Stuart

"All you have to do is 'pursue your dreams.' You hear it all the time. So why does that rarely work? *All Dreams On Deck* supplies a framework to dream expansively about your business and your life, to share dreams with those you love, and to lay the groundwork to make the dreams a reality. A must-read for anyone who wishes to get the most out of life and to achieve their dreams."

—Theresa Boyce, chair and CEO of the CEO Trust

"No matter what your dreams are, Jeremy's book will provide you with the tools to get you closer to achieving them. I have known Jeremy for 25 years, and he has lived, breathed, and developed his LifeBoat with outstanding results. I suggest you start planning your life journey today by launching your own LifeBoat."

—Don Henshall, president and CEO of Farrow & Ball

"Jeremy Cage's book, *All Dreams on Deck*, breathes life into the saying that 'if you don't know where you're going, you're never going to get there.' And Jeremy knows where he is headed. Dreams come alive in Jeremy's action-oriented manifesto—but not by accident. His book details his approach to squeezing the most from your potential (complete with worksheets to source your dreams and translate them into action), with generous helpings of insights from his successful (and occasionally less-successful) business adventures and his 'round-the-world voyage with his family. By weaving his analysis and insights with time-honored lessons on the importance of trust, intentionality, humility, listening, and rolling up your sleeves, Jeremy teaches us how to dream with one eye open. And his optimism, tethered to creating concrete plans for realizing dreams, is infectious. Get ready for a healthy dose of joy and enthusiasm while reading this book—and then get back to dreaming with a purpose that you never dreamed of before."

—Gregory D. Hess, president and professor of economics at Wabash College

JEREMY CAGE

All

DREAMS

On

DECK

CHARTING THE COURSE
for YOUR LIFE and WORK

GREENLEAF
BOOK GROUP PRESS

Published by Greenleaf Book Group Press
Austin, Texas
www.gbgpress.com

Distributed by Greenleaf Book Group

For ordering information or special discounts for bulk purchases, please contact Greenleaf Book Group at PO Box 91869, Austin, TX 78709, 512.891.6100.

Design and composition by Greenleaf Book Group
Cover design by Greenleaf Book Group

Cataloging-in-Publication data is available.

Print ISBN: 978-1-62634-338-2

eBook ISBN: 978-1-62634-339-9

Part of the Tree Neutral® program, which offsets the number of trees consumed in the production and printing of this book by taking proactive steps, such as planting trees in direct proportion to the number of trees used: www.treeneutral.com

TreeNeutral®

Printed in the United States of America on acid-free paper

16 17 18 19 20 21   10 9 8 7 6 5 4 3 2 1

First Edition

This book is dedicated to the dreamer in all of us.

———

"Men [and women] are often capable of greater things than they perform. They are sent into the world with bills of credit and seldom draw to their full extent."

—Horace Walpole

CONTENTS

Acknowledgments

I have been fortunate to have many teachers and role models throughout the course of my life. I'd like to thank all of them and call out a few folks in particular. My deepest thanks to Pat, Bradley, and Elena for all your love and support and for our exciting life together as a family. To Dad and Mum, thanks for being such wonderful role models to me in so many ways. Although he's no longer with us, many thanks to Dr. Strawn for guiding me to such a fulfilling college career. To Kevin Hall, you've been more of an inspiration, friend, and mentor to me than you'll ever know. To John O'Keefe, thanks for all your teaching, your business wisdom, and your challenge for me to keep thinking and acting "beyond the box." To Pedro Padierna, thanks for being such a terrific boss—and for being the key enabler behind my taking a sabbatical to sail the world rather than having to quit! Last but not least, thanks to all my family and friends for your unwavering support and for continuing to push me to unleash the full potential of my life.

Prepare Your LifeBoat for the Adventures of a Lifetime

Welcome aboard! It's very important as we embark on this journey together to establish some context and share a few foundational philosophies and concepts that frame the approach to life and work reflected in this book.

Life Balance, Not Work–Life Balance

The first has to do with the concept of work–life balance. So many folks spend a huge portion of their time trying to achieve the right work–life balance, and there have been volumes written on the subject. My first point is that work–life balance doesn't exist. There is *life balance*, of which work is only one part. This is **very** important. Dividing life up into two huge containers (work and life) is a dangerous oversimplification of how complex human beings are. To simplify, life balance works like this: you have many elements to your life, and you need to care for each of those elements.

Take a look at figures I.1 and I.2. Figure I.1 is obviously a scale with a pivot in the middle. On this scale, there are two big containers: *work* and *life*. If either of those gets thrown out of whack or falls off, your whole life gets thrown **way** out of balance, which thrusts you into a crisis.

Figure I.1. Work–life balance.

Figure I.2 shows a LifeBoat. A LifeBoat is critically important; it literally keeps you alive. But it will only keep you alive if it contains many important elements. At sea, some of those elements would include food rations, a device in which to catch water or make saltwater into drinkable water, flares to signal distant ships or aircraft, an emergency beacon to transmit your position, a heat-reflective blanket, a rubber repair kit in case of a puncture, and a fishing rod. A LifeBoat doesn't have everything in it; if it did, it would sink. You only have so much room, so you have to prioritize the most important things; they go in the LifeBoat first.

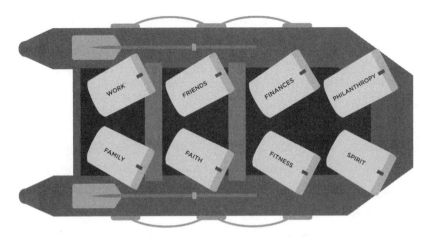

Figure I.2. LifeBoat.

And so it is with our metaphorical LifeBoat—our lives. There are many elements that more accurately reflect your unique, individual multifaceted nature, so you must determine what you need for your own LifeBoat.

A LifeBoat contains what are called Grab Bags, containers for all the supplies necessary for survival. For me, there are eight essentials for my LifeBoat: work, family, friends, faith, fitness/sports, finances, philanthropy, and spirit. I can evaluate the "health" of these elements by envisioning each inside its own Grab Bag: Is it empty or well provisioned, filling up or being used up? Using this approach, if one of the eight Grab Bags suddenly gets thrown out of whack but the other seven are in good shape, my whole life doesn't suddenly get turned upside down—and my LifeBoat doesn't sink. One-eighth of my life is out of whack, which makes it much less of a crisis and much more of a manageable challenge or issue that I can address and solve.

Everything starts with a dream. This is one of the most important concepts in the book, and I discuss this idea in detail in chapter 1. I urge you to get to a point where you can clearly articulate the dreams you have for each of the important Grab Bags in your LifeBoat.

Several years ago I was sitting down with the CEO of a large Fortune 50 company to discuss why, as the company was delivering stellar results under his leadership and the stock price was surging, he had abruptly resigned. He shared his perspective with me and calmly underscored that while the work Grab Bag was full to the brim, his family, friends, and faith Grab Bags were not as full as he'd like, because the time requirements of his job were enormous. He did not feel he could dedicate the necessary energy and time to his CEO job *and* simultaneously refill his family, friends, and faith Grab Bags.

With a focus on life balance, I believe his decision to resign was probably not overwhelmingly difficult. He chose to look at it in the context of his "whole life." He stepped into a completely different kind of role that enabled him to feel fulfilled at work but that also afforded him the time to attend to the other Grab Bags he needed to have a better life balance.

My father did something similar. He held a very senior position at a Fortune 500 company. At age fifty-three, he took stock of his work, family, and spirit Grab Bags. He had not been particularly happy for the preceding four or five years. He had always lived well below his means, and so he decided to retire early. Rather than focus the rest of his life on wealth accumulation, he determined that he had enough in that Grab Bag and wanted to focus on the other Grab Bags. He dedicated the next decade of his life to building houses for the homeless with Habitat for Humanity—actually swinging the hammer, not in some administrative role. He had found an outlet for his dream of helping others, so his spirit and philanthropy Grab Bags filled up. He had more time to spend with the family, and so that Grab Bag filled up too. As a young man starting out in my career, I was baffled at first by his decision. But with the benefit of time, it's now crystal clear.

I recognize that we're not all CEOs or senior executives who have the luxury of being able to walk away from our jobs. The point I'm trying to underscore here is that when you take the time to not only look at life balance in this multifaceted way but also *pursue* life balance in this way, it will be a key enabler to unleashing your full potential—no matter how you define it for yourself.

Adventure

The second foundational philosophy that frames how I approach my life, and this book, is that both business and life should be an adventure. *Adventure* is any unusual and exciting or daring experience. When you think about business as an adventure, it becomes a lot more exciting. Building new ways for the world to communicate; creating medicines that can transform the lives of people suffering from illnesses; creating new modes of transportation that dramatically reduce our carbon footprint; launching a new brand, product, or service; opening a pizza restaurant with the most amazing pizza on the planet—you name it, these are all adventures!

There's not a single business out there that wouldn't benefit from approaching their work as an adventure. And yet there are far too many businesses and organizations that are operating on cruise control—conducting business as usual—and avoiding failure at all costs. As I reflect on the companies I work with now, this appears especially symptomatic of really big companies. They tend to evolve into large, highly matrixed bureaucracies that are slow to plan and even slower to execute. As a result, many of them are losing market share to much nimbler, more agile, and more adventurous smaller companies.

Strategic plans, annual operating plans, disciplined marketing, innovation, and supply-chain or go-to-market planning and execution are all critically important for large companies to thrive, but they cannot be the end goal. They should all be treated as components of the business adventure—of achieving the company's dreams.

And while we're at it, why not approach life itself as "an unusual and exciting or daring experience"? As you will read, my wife and I have really embraced this philosophy. Life adventure takes many forms, and I believe that, just like any skill, the more you practice it, the better you get. The better you get at creating adventure, the more comfortable you become with adventure, which continues the cycle to make you even better at it. The better you get at adventure, the more you can apply it to all aspects of your life. It's an adventure virtuous circle—the more you do it, the better you get, and the better you get, the more you do it. And that is why, throughout the course of this book, I jump back and forth between adventures across all the different Grab Bags in the LifeBoat (life balance).

CHAPTER 1

The Most Powerful Force on the Planet

We're being bombarded by huge, breaking waves crashing in on us from all sides, trapped in a mean tropical storm that has stalled and expanded to cover the majority of the Coral Sea between New Caledonia and the Australian coast. After two harrowing days, the wind—a furious forty or fifty knots, angry and screaming at us—doesn't seem to be letting up at all. The waves are just enormous—engulfing our forty-three-foot catamaran, *Hakuna Matata*, completely from time to time as we dive into the valleys of the sea.

As we climb the face of the next wave, water cascades off the boat, once again revealing her sleek white hulls and cabin roof. Pat is doing her best to keep the kids calm and dry down below. We don't have any sails up (it's called *running under bare poles*), and yet we are being shot forward at twenty to twenty-five knots by the force of the wind and waves. At night, the sky is pitch black. The rain is essentially horizontal, biting into my face and finding a way to run down my neck under my foul-weather gear, chilling me to the bone. Radar does not work in these conditions, so we are literally sailing blind. Think of driving along a dark road at high speed with no headlights! In these conditions, there could easily be a tanker or cargo ship at the bottom of the next wave just waiting to collide with us, smash us to pieces, and send us to a watery grave.

We use our long-range single-sideband radio to contact the Australian Coast Guard every six hours, notifying them of our location, speed, and heading. If they don't hear from us every six hours, they'll know where to start looking. We are also issuing emergency calls (known as *Pan-Pans*) on our short-range VHF radio to ensure that no other boats are too close. I am on edge—we are all on edge. The storm rages on for three days and three nights. Opportunities to sleep are few. Pat and Bradley stand watch to give me some relief from time to time—but getting a deep rest is out of the question. I am absolutely exhausted! And I've never felt more alive! I've never **had** to be more alive. Our very survival depends on it.

Figure 1.1. Big waves off Hakuna Matata's stern.

These conditions, of course, were not what we experienced during most of our sixteen-month adventure sailing the world. But they were the conditions we faced during our passage across the Coral Sea as we approached the eastern coast of Australia (figure 1.1). Imagine what might have happened had we not been prepared! Sailing the world was one of our dreams. We were living it. As is the case more often than not, living our dream meant being daring and taking some risks. But from my point of view, **not** pursuing the dream posed a greater risk—the risk of a life filled with regret.

Dreams Often Involve Risk

Martin Luther King Jr. also had a dream, which, in the defining speech of his lifetime, he declared in front of an audience of millions gathered around the Lincoln Memorial in Washington, DC. His dream was for a better America, where all men, women, and children, regardless of race or ethnic origin, are judged not by the color of their skin but by the content of their character. He went on to share, in very specific detail, what America, once his dream was realized, would look like. Would feel like. Would be like.

He was passionate, energetic, bold, specific, and courageous. He gave us a vision, a voice, and a face for a better United States of America. Not only that, but he also vigorously pursued his dream with actions by organizing marches, nonviolent protests, relentless meetings with government officials, and massive rallies. His dream was also an adventure fraught with risk, and one that ultimately cost him his life. But let's take a moment to consider his alternatives.

Here again, there was also huge risk in doing nothing at all— choosing to accept the status quo. He could have followed a safer and more traditional approach, such as declaring his wishes in a letter or at a church meeting—"I have an objective"—and left it at that. Both of these options would have been significantly less risky but also significantly less effective.

By being so much less inspiring, so much less captivating, and so much less intentional, he certainly would not have ignited the level of comprehensive racial-equality reforms that he did. He would likely still be alive. But in his eighties, as he sat reflecting upon his life, I am certain he would conclude that he could have done much more to better the world. I am sure he would conclude that he was going to die full of potential, by which I mean his potential as defined by him. I'll discuss this in more detail a bit later on.

There's a fairly well-known saying, "Some men dream of worthy accomplishments, while others stay awake and do them." Aside from the inherent sexism, on the surface it's easy to nod in agreement. After all, it seems like the kind of pep talk you'd get from your coach, teacher, or parents. But I fundamentally disagree. As evidenced by our voyage and MLK Jr.'s speech, by the time we're done, I hope you'll have updated the quotation in your mind to something more like "Dreams are the most powerful force on the planet. We all dream, and we all have much more power to realize those dreams and unleash our full potential than we are using." It's time to call all dreams on deck!

A Bit about Me

I am not a scientist, at least not in the traditional sense of the word. As I began my college career at Wabash College, a small liberal arts college in Crawfordsville, Indiana, I really had no idea what I wanted to do. I knew I should go to college but really lacked any kind of direction. So during my first year, I decided to give premed and traditional science a try.

What a catastrophe! I didn't have any success with biology. It must have been readily apparent, because I remember quite vividly how my professor pulled me aside one day and asked me what I was doing in the class. He wasn't being mean; he was just baffled, because I was such a square peg in a round hole. Chemistry was even worse. My brain just isn't wired that way. I could never get those darn molecular-structure models to look like anything but modern sculpture. Physics was very much the same.

My French professor at Wabash was a relentlessly gentle and wise man named Dr. Strawn. He noticed how I was struggling with my pre-med choice and had taken the time to speak to other professors about me (the benefits and risks of a small college—people know who you are!). I remember being called to Dr. Strawn's office, where he sat me down, offered me tea, and asked me all about what was going on with my studies. Everyone was convinced I was bright, and none of the other professors understood why I was struggling so much in their classes. After a while, our discussion evolved into more of a challenge.

"Jeremy," he asked, "why don't you just study what you love? It may seem risky and may not seem to make any sense on the surface, but if you summon the courage to do that, I promise you that the rest will take care of itself."

This was profound advice that I followed and that actually changed my life. I went on to major in French, painting, and sculpture, with a minor in economics! And I thrived. I was even fortunate enough to study at the American Institute for Foreign Study at the Sorbonne in Paris. When I followed my dreams, I soared, and as it turns out, I believe that my new path equipped me perfectly to be a different kind of scientist.

Scientists study things. They study every aspect of our fascinating world—everything in it, and everything that surrounds it. They take what they have learned and use it to advance their thinking—and to advance their science. They develop hypotheses, then run tests and conduct experiments to prove whether they are right or wrong. Using this broader definition, I am most definitely a scientist.

I have lived and worked in England, Germany, France, Belgium, Sweden, Venezuela, Brazil, Mexico, and the United States. I have studied and learned about the people who live in these places: who they are, what's important to them and why, what gets them excited, what drives them crazy, their cultures, their traditions. And it's exciting.

In terms of a profession, I have spent thirty years of my life working in what is commonly referred to as the "consumer goods industry." Broadly speaking, that means understanding people's needs, figuring out which of their needs are not being met, and developing innovation and marketing solutions to address those unmet needs. Then, of course, it also means persuading them to buy more of our product than of our competition's!

Succeeding in consumer goods means not only seeing the tip of the iceberg of consumer behavior but also understanding what lies beneath the surface. You do this by using a *combination of facts and intuition*, which leads you to develop innovations that are both highly relevant (meaningful to the consumer) and highly distinctive (different from all the other products or services on the market).

Big breakthroughs often meet needs that people didn't even know they had. No one was specifically asking for an online resource where they could buy their music (iTunes); or for a machine that would enable them to play games and solve problems (the computer); or for a way to make their music portable (the Sony Walkman); or for a minicomputer that they could take everywhere (smartphones, iPads); or for a motorized vehicle to replace their horse; or for an alternative way to take a taxi (Uber); or for a way to find out or find *anything* using a computer (the Internet); or for a way to instantly know their precise location

(GPS); or for a way to instantly update everyone on where they are and what they're doing (Facebook, Twitter). These are all hugely successful ventures that many of us now can't imagine living without. And most of them are the result of understanding what lies "beneath the surface."

So while I'm a practical scientist, not an academic scientist, here's my emphatic scientific declaration: *Dreams are the most powerful force on our planet.*

Nurturing Your Dreams

Take a few minutes to really think and reflect on the life that immediately surrounds you. Let's go from big to small. The United States of America started as a dream—a land of opportunity where men and women could live with freedom of speech, freedom of religion, with liberty and justice for all. From this dream, literally millions of different industries were formed.

The car you drive started with a dream: Henry Ford had a dream to bring automotive transportation to the masses, and we've never looked back. Your parents' marriage or relationship started with the dream of a loving, happy life together, and you were part of that dream. The phone you use, the TV you watch, the GPS you use, Facebook, Twitter, Google, iTunes all started with a dream. You get the picture. Almost everything that touches your life today, even your very existence, started with a dream. Truly, dreams are the most powerful force on the planet.

As children, we are full of dreams. "I want to be this when I grow up." "I want to do that." But something seems to happen as we go through school, then college, and then adulthood. Our daily lives, both at work and at home, just get so busy that many of our dreams get put on the back burner. We promise ourselves that we'll get around to them one day, but that day just keeps getting pushed out.

Stephen Covey, the famous author of *The Seven Habits of Highly Effective People*, now in its anniversary edition (New York: Simon & Schuster, 2013), and other books, has a wonderful exercise called "Rock, Sand, and Water" that illustrates this point perfectly. If you take a jar and fill it first with all the small stuff (sand), there won't be any room for the big stuff (rocks; figure 1.2). If you start the other way around—putting the rocks in first—there's plenty of room for all the small stuff (sand) to fit around them.

Figure 1.2. Putting the small stuff first means the big stuff doesn't fit.

Think of the rocks as the most important dreams in your LifeBoat. Nothing is typically more energizing or more powerful. Yet all too often, we fill our lives with so much of the small stuff first that our dreams get squeezed out. There's just not enough room.

That's what many of us do to ourselves. As if that isn't enough, often friends, family members, or colleagues don't take our dreams seriously and may even poke fun at them. They don't believe in you or your dreams, so over time, many of those dreams simply get discarded.

Finally, and equally as upsetting, far too many of us have simply given up. For all the good that there is in this world, there continues to be far too much hardship. Many people have struggled in their personal lives through financial crises, unemployment, broken relationships, tragedies, crimes, addictions, and unrewarding jobs or careers. We hear nothing but bad news on the TV: violence and wars, global warming—you name it. Who has time for dreams and adventure?

The same applies to business. As I look around today, and work with Fortune 500 clients across multiple industries, it is clear that many leaders have forgotten how to effectively articulate the dreams of the company and instead have replaced them with boring old objectives—a far less inspiring way to say the same thing. When company leaders can clearly articulate their dream and can keep everyone focused on delivering that dream, their company soars.

Look at Procter & Gamble (P&G), the maker of such ubiquitous brands as Tide, Crest, Pantene, Head & Shoulders, CoverGirl, Oil of Olay, and so on. Their dream is "to provide products and services of superior quality and value that improve the lives of all the world's consumers, every day." If they do that well, which they have for most of their history, people buy more. Revenue goes up. Innovations are launched. Profits go up. The communities in which they live and work prosper. And shareholders are happy. For P&G, that has been the case for the vast majority of their time in business since the founding of the company in 1837. When a company fails to articulate its dream, it's all too easy for the associates to lose sight of the dream, and they tend to get in trouble.

What are the takeaways here? Quite simply, that dreams are incredibly powerful—the most powerful force on the planet. And yet, they are simultaneously incredibly vulnerable. If not prioritized, protected, and nurtured, they can easily wither away and die.

Unrealized Potential

That leads me to a few more scientific claims. First, we are all going to die. The last time I checked, the rate of death has held steady at one hundred percent. Second, the vast majority of us, no matter how successful we have been up to now, will die full of potential. And the vast majority of businesses will also die full of potential.

In the case of unforeseen tragedies—illnesses, accidents, violence—it is easier for us to wrap our minds around the concept of people dying full of potential. When we lose people too young and too soon, it's inevitable. But what about a life fully lived to old age (whatever that's defined as today). Why is it that so many of us live so long and yet still die full of potential? There's a disconnect. One would naturally assume that the longer we live, the more of our potential we'll realize. But it's just not the case. So what's the real driver of realizing your full potential? It lies not only in the power of your dreams but, critically, also in the actions you are taking (or not taking) to bring them to life.

My father-in-law passed away when he was ninety. He was a wonderful, kindhearted man who had been married for almost sixty-five years and raised a wonderful daughter whom I love dearly. He and my mother-in-law were real trailblazers when it came to international travel. They took delivery of a VW Bug in Europe in 1967, well before it was a common thing to do. They then explored the continent in an era when very few people spoke English, armed with little more than hand gestures and sign language! They explored the Soviet Union well before the wall came down. They explored China way before there was any infrastructure for Western tourists.

My father-in-law led a very full life. Yet he would occasionally sit with me and talk about all the ideas that he had had during the course of his life. He even kept notes—a sketchbook to capture his ideas. He "invented" an awful lot of products well before they were actually brought to market—by someone else. Even though he had led a very full and successful life, my father-in-law died full of potential, as he defined it for himself.

This is important for me to reiterate here—I am not advocating that everybody has to dream about being a CEO or a president or an Olympic gold medalist. When I am talking about realizing your full potential, I am referring to the potential you define for yourself. Many people will have an opinion, and many will help you along the way, but ultimately, you and you alone can judge what you believe to be your full potential, and therefore you and you alone can assess whether you're leaving that potential on the table!

• • •

As it relates to business, it's often easier to see companies that have died full of potential or that continue to exist but are clearly not realizing their full potential. When I began my tenure as CEO of a struggling lighting-technology company full of potential, the company was rudderless. For a variety of reasons, changes in leadership at the company had been almost nonstop, which left all the associates screaming for some direction. There was no trust and a huge amount of political infighting. There was no dream, there was no team, and the company's poor results reflected that.

One of the very first things I did was to rearticulate the company's dream, to remind all people in the organization that the reason they came to work every day was "to unleash the science of light to make people and our planet look, feel, and heal better." There were many things wrong with the company, but one of the most fundamental that needed to be addressed was that everyone had lost sight of the dream. Everyone was so caught up in internal politics, changes in leadership, the company's poor financial health, the lack of clear strategies and plans, and the lack of effective processes that the dream had been forgotten. And this is a problem that's all too common. When institutions—schools, companies, organizations, or whatever—fail to keep everyone focused on the dream, history has proven that most of them will fail.

Saab Automobile is a business whose death while still full of potential has been well documented. Saab had been a very successful car company for most of its seventy-year history. As late as the 1980s their anchor vehicle, the Saab 900, was just as desirable as similar offerings from BMW, Audi, and Mercedes. Following GM's takeover of the business in 1989, the company, its associates, and ultimately the consumer lost sight of the dream. They embarked upon an extensive effort to cut costs and standardize the chassis with other GM brands such as Opel and Vauxhall.

Instead of making distinctive, quirky Swedish cars bursting with "premium" and personality, their cars became bland upgrades of standard GM cars. The company's associates were confused. So were consumers. They no longer perceived Saab as being a viable alternative to other luxury brands. According to a *Forbes* article written by Stephen Pope in December 2011, sales peaked at about 133,000 cars in 2006. They sold 31,700 cars in 2010.[1] GM sold the business in 2010 for next to nothing to Spyker, which declared bankruptcy in 2011. National Electric Vehicle Sweden bought Saab in 2012—with hopes to bring the brand back to life someday.

Another example of a company that lost its focus is Eastman Kodak. The Eastman Company was formed in 1889[2] by George Eastman—and

---

1   Stephen Pope, "So Long SAAB, This Time It Is Over," *Forbes*,
     December 19, 2011, http://www.forbes.com/sites/stephenpope/2011/12/19/
     so-long-saab-this-time-it-is-over/#1b17805b1078.
2   Kodak, "Birth of a Company," http://www.kodak.com/ek/us/en/corp/aboutus/
     heritage/georgeeastman/default.htm.

what a fantastic adventure it was. George's dream was to make photography and cameras as easy to use as a pencil. All consumers had to do was point the camera and press a button. Kodak would do the rest—namely take the roll of film, develop it, and you'd get back your pictures in return.

With a strong focus on research and development, quality, and never losing sight of the dream, revenue for the company one hundred years after being founded was $10 billion.[3] But the company lost sight of their dream. They actually invented the digital camera in 1975[4]—which really is as easy to use as a pencil. Despite digital being a better solution for consumers, Kodak did not commercialize the technology because it threatened their highly lucrative business model of developing film. Competitors adapted fast—essentially rendering the incumbent business model obsolete.

Kodak made some bad strategic choices and thus failed to adapt quickly enough from traditional cameras and film developing to address the needs of the market. A company that boasted revenues of $19 billion in 1990, employed 145,000 associates, and was ranked as the fifth most valuable brand in the world today has around 8,000 employees and revenues of around $2 billion[5] and makes no money. The company declared bankruptcy in 2012.

Of course these are not the only two examples of companies dying full of potential. Another is Radio Shack—a company focused on electronics in an electronics-focused world. They lost their way, and went out of business in 2015. Will JCPenney, Sears, and Kmart be next?

---

3   PhotoSecrets, "The Rise & Fall of Kodak: A Brief History of the Eastman Kodak Company, 1880 to 2012," http://photosecrets.com/the-rise-and-fall-of-kodak.

4   Ibid.

5   Ben Geier, "This Is Kodak's New Plan to Stay Afloat," *Fortune*, March 20, 2015, http://fortune.com/2015/03/20/kodak-patents/.

Are any of these historical powerhouses on their way out because they have lost sight of their dream or have failed to adapt to the changing needs of the market? These resonate because they are names we know, and they make the evening news. Not making the evening news are the thousands of smaller or regional businesses that die full of potential every single day—the small local companies, the start-ups, the farms—you name it. These companies employ about fifty percent of the private-sector workforce in the United States—and yet (depending on the source), somewhere around ninety percent of all new businesses fail.

To be clear, I'm not suggesting that every business should succeed. There are an awful lot of companies that do not have the right to succeed. For some, their products are relevant but not distinctive—so they are essentially a commodity. Commodities tend to sell on price—meaning the cheaper it is, the more you sell. The problem with that is the big guys already have scale advantage and cost advantage, so it's almost impossible to compete with them and actually make money.

Other companies offer products or services that are distinctive but not relevant. These are essentially a fad. Fads come and go—some quicker than others. If the business model is designed to get in quick and get out quick, then fads can be very lucrative. The problem arises when founders don't actually plan for their company to be a fad. They build a big infrastructure, planning for strong long-term sales—which never materialize.

A final group of start-ups offers products or services that are neither distinctive nor relevant. They fail, and they should. The vast majority of the companies that went bust following the Internet boom in the 1990s failed because they were not offering a meaningful benefit to consumers. Their founders simply wanted to hop on the bandwagon and make some money.

Realized Potential

The companies whose dreams were focused on the consumer or customer and on providing them with a superior experience or a meaningful new experience thrived then—and, to a great extent, thrive to this day.

Amazon was founded in 1994 as a company that offered consumers a more convenient way to buy and read books. However, Jeff Bezos, the company's founder and CEO, understood that they had a lot of unrealized potential and has since embarked on the adventure of fundamentally transforming the way the world shops. Today the company employs about 231,000 employees and has revenues of about $100 billion.[6]

Mark Zuckerberg established Facebook in 2004 essentially to help college students find others to date—a way to help people connect with one another. However, he understood that the company had a lot of unrealized potential and has since led his company on the adventure of fundamentally transforming the way the world communicates. Today Facebook has about 1.5 billion users across the world and employs about 12,500 people.[7]

Dreams are not theoretical. They are real. And, as I indicated earlier, they often involve risk. I invite you to reflect deeply on your dreams, to reignite the passion for the ones you really care about, and I'll challenge you to bring them to life—regardless of whether you are just starting your career, midway through life, or retired, whether you're a student, a stay-at-home mom or dad, or an executive leading a big business. Dreams apply to all of us, and they apply to all aspects of our lives.

---

6   Ángel González, "Amazon on Pace to Boast Fortune 500's Second-Largest Workforce," *Seattle Times*, updated February 20, 2016, http://www.seattletimes.com/business/amazon/amazon-on-pace-to-boast-fortune-500s-second-largest-workforce/.

7   "Facebook," Wikipedia, last modified March 2, 2016, https://en.wikipedia.org/wiki/Facebook.

CHART YOUR COURSE

As we dig in, please grab a pencil and flip to page 141 in the back of the book. Now is the time to begin charting the course for your life and work. To do so, you must first figure out where you are going, and what you value. The first exercise (p. 142) is to determine the most important elements of your life—your Grab Bags. The second exercise (pp. 143–145) is to take *at least* fifteen minutes to list your dreams off the top of the top of your head and to determine which are the most important to you. Don't skimp on this exercise. It should be the one that you prioritize above all others.

CHAPTER 2

Dream Like You Mean It

The sun was shining with just a few puffy clouds dancing through the sky. The mainsail and genoa were filled. We had actually made it all the way across the Atlantic Ocean, through the Caribbean, and through the Panama Canal. We were now in the Pacific. Wow! The fishing line was out, and the tuna were biting. All seemed well with the world. The magnificent Galapagos Islands were about six hundred miles away, but as it turns out, they might as well have been on the other side of the world! After numerous days at sea, we simply could not make any meaningful progress toward our destination. Using our single-sideband (long-distance) radio, we radioed our friends Teri and Lee aboard their thirty-seven-foot sailboat—heading to the same destination as us.

"*Glendora, Glendora*, this is *Hakuna Matata*. How is everything aboard? Are you making any progress toward the Galapagos? Over."

"*Hakuna*, this is *Glendora*. All's well on board—except for our progress. This is the most frustrating passage! It doesn't feel as though we're going anywhere. Over."

"Have you heard from any other boats? Is there better wind to the south? Over."

"We've heard from *Paramour* and *Stargazer*. Apparently they have better wind, but the current against them there is even stronger, so they're not making any progress either. Over."

"Okay. Guess we'll hang in there. Keep us posted on your progress. This is *Hakuna* switching over to VHF channel 16. Over and out."

Dream Specifically

There's a concept in sailing called *velocity made good*, or VMG for short. Because a sailboat cannot point directly into the wind and make any forward progress, you have to sail at an angle to the wind. So VMG is the speed that you're actually making toward your destination. Our VMG to the Galapagos was simply awful! Everything looked great on the surface, but there were forces holding us back. The most obvious was that the wind was coming directly from where we wanted to go.

To make any forward progress, we had to sail at a forty-degree angle to the wind (called *tacking*), so we were doing a massive zigzag toward our destination. That quickly turns a six-hundred-mile passage into a twelve-hundred-mile passage. The wind was also unseasonably light, so we just weren't sailing fast enough.

However, perhaps the most disheartening force working against us was the one we couldn't see. There were strong currents under the surface of the sea that were literally pushing us back toward Panama. So while the boat felt as though she was moving forward across the surface of the ocean, we were actually making very little progress.

The same thing has a tendency to occur in our day-to-day lives: Our VMG just isn't good enough. We have our eyes on a goal, or a dream, and yet there are forces—both seen and unseen—working against our realizing those dreams.

A key question to ask yourself to begin counteracting those forces is this: Do I really know where I am heading, and where I want to go? Said another way—how am I dreaming?

Back in 1987 when I was just beginning my career at Procter & Gamble, I was jogging with a dear friend of mine, Kevin, during our lunch break. We would cover all sorts of topics—ranging from work to sports, his family, politics, you name it—as we jogged through the streets of Cincinnati and northern Kentucky. One day, out of the blue, he challenged me with a few deep questions.

"So"—he said between breaths—"what do you want to be when you grow up?" He didn't ask it condescendingly; it was just a friendly way to ask a serious question that he had recently been posed by another senior P&G executive named John O'Keeffe.

I replied with a deeply insightful grunt and said, "Successful, I guess."

"Well, what does that mean?"

"I want to do well at work, want a great personal life, want to travel—you know, the usual." I think at this point we may have slowed to a walk.

"Well, do you want to leave it down to dumb luck?"

"Of course not."

"Then you need to get serious about how you're dreaming!"

He suggested that one of the most fundamental reasons that so many people and businesses will die full of potential is that we dream all wrong.

"How are you dreaming?" Kevin asked again. "If you've just got some vague dream of what it is you want to be or do, then I guarantee that all sorts of obstacles, fears, and dreads are going to paralyze you and prevent you from achieving that dream."

What does this really mean? If you are like most folks—like I was during that run with Kevin—you have a dream. In fact, you have lots of dreams, and yet, the chances are that they are not specific at all. Almost by default, our VMG toward them will be poor.

Dreams—in every section of your LifeBoat—like wanting to be successful in business, wanting to retire rich or early, wanting to be happier, or wanting to have a strong marriage are all vague. Each is lacking specific detail about not only how you'll arrive at that goal but also what the dream specifically means. What does it mean to you to be happy? How much do you require in your savings account to fund a comfortable retirement? "I want to have a successful career" is a dream that almost everyone has, but people who are specific about defining what success means to them, how they will get there, and by when are far more likely to achieve the dream.

Without specifics, all these dreams lack "teeth"; they are vague. And because they are vague, they open the door for you to focus on the obstacles, fears, and dreads. Pat and I could quite easily have articulated the dream of sailing around the world with our kids someday. Keeping it that vague would have resulted in a paralyzing number of specific obstacles, fears, and dreads: We're putting the family in danger; we're not skilled enough; taking a long break could stall my career; the kids might get behind at school; we would be unpaid for eighteen months yet still need to cover the mortgage and other expenses; the cost of a seaworthy boat is pretty high; and so on. Our dream would have been sunk before we'd even begun! It happens all the time.

Let's bring this to life by reaching into the LifeBoat and using the dream of early retirement. In the dream-vaguely scenario, the conversation goes something like this: "I'd really love to retire early, but I've got to pay for the kids to go to college. I've got to pay off the house. I'll drive my spouse crazy. I don't know where we'd live. I don't have enough interests outside of work. I probably don't have enough money saved up. Will it last? I don't know what I'd do if my friends are all still working." And the list of objections, obstacles, and dreads goes on and on.

Ultimately, these negatives get so overwhelming that they paralyze you and prevent you from ever achieving your dream. Your VMG toward that dream will stall altogether, and the likelihood is high that you won't achieve it. That's what I mean when I say you'll die full of potential. You could have achieved something that was important to you during the course of your lifetime, but you didn't.

Back to the theory of VMG. You are not always sailing against a current when you set sail, and you do not always have to tack back and forth because the wind is coming directly from your destination. Sometimes, the wind is on your beam, (coming across the side of the boat). This typically enables your boat to sail along nice and fast. And sometimes, the current is actually accelerating your progress toward your destination. Your boat's instruments indicate you are sailing along at seven knots, but your VMG—because of the current—is actually twelve. That doesn't sound like much of a difference for a car—but in a sailboat, it is massive, cutting the time to your destination almost in half—a really big deal! It's the difference between taking eighteen days to cross the Atlantic and taking ten and a half days. Metaphorically, this is precisely what happens when you change the way you dream. Instead of dreaming in a way that enables all your specific fears, dreads, and obstacles to paralyze you, you need to *dream specifically*. With this approach, you will be much better equipped to simply deal with all the fears, dreads, and obstacles—one at a time as they arise.

This changes the conversation entirely. The specific questions you need to answer to define and achieve that dream now look something like this: "It's really important to me that I retire early. What does *retire early* really mean for me? What age will I be? So, what year will I retire? How do I want to spend my time? Who do I want to spend my time with? How much money will I need to have saved to support the lifestyle I'm seeking in retirement? How much do I have now? Knowing that, how much do I need to save? How should I invest it, and what kind of return do I need to generate? What does that mean I have to save on a monthly basis? Is that how much I am saving?"

In this example, the course of action actually becomes quite binary (assuming that availability of money is the key enabler). If your savings are on track, keep at it, and you can make the dream happen. According to multiple sources, at the time of this printing, about half of all American households have no retirement accounts—with about one-third of all households having neither retirement savings nor a pension. Yikes! So, if you are not on track, you can either choose to increase the amount you are saving each month, or change to a more aggressive investment strategy to achieve your dream. Either that or you simply have to change what your dream of early retirement means.

With answers to these types of detailed questions, the specific dream would sound more like this: "My dream is to retire at age fifty-eight, and I want to spend most of my time 'giving back'—building homes for the homeless. I will have $X in the bank to fund my retirement, which will enable my spouse and me to live in the style we'd like until we're ninety. Right now, we're not saving enough, so to make the dream a reality, I will need to save $Y per month between now and then."

One of the positive side effects of this approach is that it places you much more firmly in the driver's seat. You have made a specific choice about what early retirement means for you, and you are taking the necessary steps to make it happen. You are no longer a victim of circumstance. You may decide to move into a smaller house, or move to an area where real estate is cheaper to reduce your mortgage—and thus be able to save at the required monthly rate. You may decide to keep your car, rather than replacing it for a new one every three years—the average frequency with which Americans change their cars. This is expensive (and is also why I am driving a well-taken-care-of sixteen-year-old car). All of these more difficult decisions will be easier because they have context—they are all enablers for you to achieve your specific dream.

My Dream to Live and Work Internationally

Let's jump into my LifeBoat. I had—and still have—lots of dreams. After college, one of my big dreams was to live and work internationally. For this, I thank my parents. My father started his career as a farmer in England. However, he did not have enough money to own a farm of his own, and he felt like he could be doing much more than he was. He left the farm and joined a few companies in their agricultural sales divisions before finding the right fit with Elanco, a division of Eli Lilly Pharmaceuticals. We followed Dad's career from London, England (where I was born, incidentally), to Frankfurt, Germany; Paris, France; Brussels, Belgium; and ultimately, to Indianapolis, Indiana, the company's global headquarters.

The original plan had been for us to be in the United States only for a few years and then head back to Europe, but once the company saw what they had in my dad, they kept promoting him, and we stayed even after he retired about a decade later. Thanks to all this moving around and traveling, I became enamored with the idea of living and working in different countries, learning new languages, and immersing myself in different cultures.

At the time Kevin challenged me to be more specific about my dreams, I was working as an assistant brand manager at Procter & Gamble's headquarters in Cincinnati, Ohio. Because P&G operates in almost all countries across the globe, I felt confident that my choice to work at P&G was the right one for making my dream of living and working in other countries come true. I sat down with my manager and the folks in human resources to get specific. Together, we mapped out a career plan that had me working internationally in four years.

Now, big companies are not travel agencies, so to work in other countries, the first thing I had to prove to P&G was that I could add value in other markets and that it would be worth the considerable investment to send me there. This simply meant that I had to consistently exceed my objectives and go above and beyond what was expected of me—both in "building the business" and in "building the organization." After doing this repeatedly for my first three years there, my business dreams and adventures started to come alive.

BALTIMORE

My first posting outside Cincinnati was supposed to have been Paris. However, a last-minute change of company plans found me in Baltimore, Maryland, as part of the first team to move to the Noxell Corporation, which P&G had just acquired. I was still pretty junior at the time, but the company's specific dream was to enable a smooth integration of the two businesses within two years of acquisition, while delivering all the usual business goals.

To achieve this, P&G sent a team of people at every level who had strong collaboration skills into Noxell to help—rather than stall progress (which so often happens in acquisitions). I won't claim the assignment was a smooth one. There was a lot of "organ rejection" of the P&G folks at first because our cultures were very different, but I like to think we helped enable a better transition through the way we interacted with the teams there and the way I managed my portion of the business. Incidentally, this turned out to be a terrific assignment, because Baltimore is where I met my wife, Pat—but we'll get to that dream in a while!

SWEDEN

After just over a year in Baltimore, I was transferred to Stockholm, Sweden, to manage several of P&G's health and beauty care brands across Sweden, Finland, Denmark, and Norway. TV advertising had just been legalized in Sweden, so the business was experiencing explosive growth. This first international assignment was a rich period of cultural learning for me and of building the capabilities of a rapidly growing subsidiary.

When I arrived in Stockholm, the office was just as busy at ten o'clock at night as it was at ten in the morning. I am a big believer in the theory that you build businesses through your people, so the more capable and empowered they are, the more successful you will be. We were hiring lots of really energetic, bright, and dedicated people, but we weren't equipping them with the skills they needed to do the job efficiently. We also had the added complication of a workforce with four completely different languages and cultures—all conveniently wrapped up into one region on the organizational chart called Scandinavia! I therefore made capability building a cornerstone of the strategic plan for the marketing and consumer insights teams.

My specific dream was to equip the team with the skills and capabilities to effectively and efficiently manage the business, without the need for outside help (in the form of expats), and to deliver a meaningful advance within the first eighteen months. We allocated a disproportionate amount of money to training and agreed from the outset that the funding could not be cut for any reason. With a high level of senior management support, I led the creation of a best-in-class training and development program, which leveraged all the resources available back at our European headquarters in London and global headquarters in Cincinnati.

What a huge transformation! The people grew, and of course, the business grew. It was hard to break everyone from the late-night habit, though. I ended up resorting to literally turning off the lights at the office no later than 8 p.m. every night to get people to go home to their friends and loved ones!

THE UNITED KINGDOM

After four rewarding years in Sweden, we were off to London, where I was responsible for consolidating all the company's various fine-fragrance brands (Hugo Boss, Giorgio Beverly Hills, and Laura Biagiotti) into one Fine Fragrance division for the company called EuroCos. Our specific dream here was to harness the strengths of the Procter & Gamble culture, the P&G UK cosmetics and fragrances culture, and the Giorgio Beverly Hills culture to double revenue and profit in three years (the "strategic planning cycle").

I would give myself a C on this one. We grew both the revenue and the profit of this entrepreneurial business by sixty percent in just two years, but despite my best efforts, I failed to really harness the strengths of the different cultures. One of P&G's cultural strengths is the discipline with which the sales force develops strong, fact-based conceptual selling materials to make the sale. I failed to get the Giorgio team to really embrace this. One of Giorgio's cultural strengths was relationship selling. I failed to get the P&G team to embrace this. Had I done a better job, we would have been a better team, and I am sure our business results would have been far better than those we actually delivered.

This will happen to you too. Things will not always go according to plan in your LifeBoat. What is critical, though, is how you react when that happens. You can blame everybody else, but if you do, you won't learn, and you are destined to repeat your mistakes. I'd strongly suggest you simply take responsibility, figure out what went wrong and why, and do better the next time. As sailors often say, "Don't turn back. Adjust the sails!"

Beyond work, this was a wonderful time for us to be on my home soil. We lived in the heart of the exciting city of London; we used London as a base for traveling all over Europe; we cruised in our Pacific Seacraft 24 sailboat, *Pourquoi Pas*, along the southern coast of the United Kingdom and across to both the Channel Islands and France; Pat got to meet and know all my relatives; and this is when we started our family. Bradley was born in London just six months prior to our move to Caracas, Venezuela.

VENEZUELA

There were a million reasons not to move to Venezuela, ranging from crime to political instability, but there was one really powerful reason to go: It was clearly going to be an adventure and was part of our dream. What a marvelous country, and what a shame that a country so rich in natural resources had eighty percent of the population living in abject poverty then.[8]

At the time, P&G's Latin American headquarters were located in Caracas. My first business challenge was to turn around the growth and profitability of the company's highly fragmented Personal Cleansing (soap) business for the region. The Personal Cleansing division was a big business, comprising many brands and factories that had become part of P&G through acquisitions. We made every size and shape of soap bar you can imagine. We even had ten different colors of white.

The factories were running well below capacity, so my specific business dream was to maintain revenue and double profit by the end

---

8   "Venezuela Population Below the Poverty Line," Index Mundi, updated June 30, 2015, http://www.indexmundi.com/g/g.aspx?c=ve&v=69.

of the three-year strategic planning cycle, despite selling some brands and discontinuing many others. By focusing on three distinctly different brands for Latin America (Zest, Safeguard, and Camay) and by standardizing and simplifying brands and manufacturing across the continent, we were indeed able to stabilize revenue and quadruple profit in just two years.

My second business challenge while living in Venezuela was to accelerate the sales and profit growth of two of the largest shampoo and conditioner brands in Latin America—Pantene and Head & Shoulders. The specific dream was to increase revenue and profit of these two brands by thirty percent at a minimum over the course of the three-year strategic plan. After a lot of analysis, it was clear that what we needed first was a much deeper level of consumer understanding in each Latin culture than we had at the time. There are many tremendous benefits of globalization, but if you lose touch with the local consumer, you are in trouble—and that's where we were.

The deeper consumer understanding agenda that we put in place unlocked some powerful insights that, in turn, led to much more effective advertising, marketing, and innovation plans. We were able to grow sales of the first brand by sixty percent. Sales of the second brand grew by fifty-six percent, and the profit of the two brands combined increased more than seventy percent.

On the personal side, just as we had imagined, this assignment also afforded us the opportunity to explore an absolutely fascinating country and culture. Venezuela has a magnificent Caribbean coastline, wide open plains, tropical rain forest, and staggering *tepuis*—vertical-sided mountains that tower into the sky. Venezuela will always be near and dear to our hearts, not only for all our travel experiences and the friends we made, but also because this was the birthplace of our daughter, Elena.

BRAZIL

Sao Paulo, Brazil, was our next destination. We moved there to continue to execute the specific business dream we had established in Caracas: unlocking the growth potential of the hair-care business in Latin America's Southern Cone (Brazil, Argentina, and Chile). We were successful in both Argentina and Chile but failed to meet our objectives in Brazil. The company needed to make some priority decisions between categories, and funding unexpectedly decreased by over ninety percent for hair care. Yikes!

Again—it is highly likely that this is going to happen to you at some point. You are going to be leading a project that suddenly gets canceled; you are going to be working at a company that suddenly goes bankrupt. If you step back and look at your LifeBoat and realize that only one Grab Bag has been thrown out of whack—then you'll be better positioned to respond.

Faced with this new reality, I contacted a mentor back at Cincinnati headquarters and asked him to either reinstate the funding I needed to do the job or find me a new assignment. He chose the latter! So before we knew it, we were off on another adventure. Beyond the business challenge, here again, we immersed ourselves in a vibrant, friendly culture, rich in history and traditions. We were able to explore the rain forest, the Pantanal, Sao Paulo, Rio de Janeiro, Parati, Salvador, and Natal. We were only in Brazil for a short time but were committed to getting the most from the experience.

BACK TO THE UNITED STATES

Upon returning to the United States, I assumed responsibility for Head & Shoulders and Pert Plus—two huge, very mature brands. The specific dream for one was to deliver above-market growth as soon as the next fiscal year. The specific dream for the other was to reverse a multiyear decline without sacrificing profitability. Improving the effectiveness of advertising, addressing issues with in-store execution, and focusing the organization on three key product initiatives resulted in over twenty percent growth of Head & Shoulders. By refocusing advertising and marketing against the base Pert Plus business, we were successfully able to reverse a fifteen percent revenue decline, while simultaneously increasing profit.

While things on the business front were going well and I was exceeding my objectives, I became very frustrated with the size of the company and bureaucracy of being back at the US headquarters. I was also frustrated by the politics and the lack of mentors I had in Cincinnati. Reflecting on that later (and with the wisdom that comes from age, I guess), I think my lack of mentors in Cincinnati was a failure on my part.

At the time, I blamed it on having been living and working internationally for so long. I figured it was a consequence of my dream that I should have just accepted. Sure, I thought to myself, I could have fostered mentors in Cincinnati had I stayed there throughout my career, but that's not what I wanted to do. As I look back, I realize that I had built a strong mentor network internationally, but I should have also invested more time and emotional capital in building stronger mentor and sponsor relationships throughout the company. I somewhat naively thought that my work was enough—and that it would speak for itself. As Carla Harris, the vice chairman at Morgan Stanley, so succinctly put it in a speech I recently heard her give—"Work can't speak. Only humans can!!" Had I invested more time and effort in this area, it's possible that I would have stayed at P&G longer than I did.

But I didn't. After sixteen very fulfilling years—both professionally and personally—I resigned from P&G even though this was not part of my original plan or dream. There are always going to be things that happen that are unexpected. When it's something as big as leaving a company, I'd suggest it's time to pull out your list of dreams and your LifeBoat, and reassess. Are they still the right dreams? Are you living off old dreams? What has changed? Spend the time to rearticulate and update your dreams, and often you'll find these big transitions can act as springboards to achieving the future you seek.

• • •

And that's what happened to me. I left P&G to become a vice president managing some consumer brands for Schering-Plough Healthcare (such as Dr. Scholl's). I was attracted by the business challenge and also by the idea of being a bigger fish in a smaller pond. However, a lot of negative things hit the company during the two months between my leaving P&G and joining Schering-Plough that dramatically altered not only my job but also the future of the business. So, by my own choosing, my tenure there ended up being very short.

MEXICO AND THE UNITED STATES

While still working at Schering-Plough, I was approached by the president of PepsiCo International. After a very exciting meeting with him, and after meeting more members of the company's leadership team, I joined the company, and we were back on another adventure—this time to Mexico. The business challenge was terrific and, from a professional standpoint, was probably the most fun I've had in my career. I was also fortunate enough to have an incredible boss who had a lot to teach me and who trusted me completely.

The Sabritas business in Mexico (Lay's, Doritos, Cheetos, Ruffles, and many local brands) was the largest snack business PepsiCo had outside North America, and growth had stalled. The specific dream was to immediately reignite the business and deliver above-market revenue growth after a few years of stagnation. The root cause of our business issue was that headquarters had been pressuring the Sabritas business for more profit over a period of several years—to make up for profit shortfalls elsewhere in PepsiCo International. To achieve this, the company had increased the prices of our brands too aggressively—to the point where the price that consumers thought they should be paying for our brands was much less than the actual asking price.

When this happens, consumers don't think they are getting a good value. You have broken the consumer value equation, and growth stalls—or worse yet, declines. You would feel great about paying for a Chevrolet and getting a Cadillac. You would feel bad about paying for a Cadillac and getting a Chevrolet! To address this, we developed and executed marketing innovations and product innovations that significantly increased the perceived value of our brands (the price consumers thought they should pay for our brands), thus fixing our broken value equation. We also focused heavily on training to equip the organization to do more, do it better, and do it more efficiently. Together, these actions enabled us to quickly reignite the growth of the business and increase sales by over thirty percent in a four-year period.

The people of Mexico are some of the happiest in the world, according to the Happy Planet Index (http://www.happyplanetindex. org/), a project of the new economics foundation, despite the fact that many of them have very little in the way of financial resources. I am intentionally not calling them poor, because they are rich in many ways that really matter—love, friendship, happiness, cultural heritage. The adventure of immersing ourselves in Mexico's culture has provided these priceless lessons for our children, who are continuously bombarded with the importance placed on material goods and status here in the United States.

My second assignment at PepsiCo was chief marketing officer of the International Foods business based out of New York. Here, my specific dream was to accelerate global sales and share growth through a more powerful and more aligned or synchronized marketing and innovation agenda than the company had up until then.

My third assignment (still in New York) was senior vice president of Insights and Innovation for the North American beverage business—where my challenge was to create a much stronger long-term innovation pipeline to help accelerate sales and market-share growth of the company's beverage brands.

My fourth, and final, assignment at PepsiCo was senior vice president of the Global Snacks group—charged with developing the overall strategy, marketing, and innovation plans for the company's ~$30 billion (at the time) snacks business.

After ten very rewarding years at PepsiCo, I felt as though it was time for a change to get me back on a strong learning curve—and so I accepted the position of chief executive officer of The Lighting Science Group—a massive turnaround challenge that I referenced earlier and discuss in more detail later in the book.

Upon exiting Lighting Science, I embarked upon another adventure, fulfilling another LifeBoat dream of starting my own company—The Cage Group. Our specific dream is focused on "unleashing the full potential of businesses and people throughout the world with breakthrough strategy, marketing, and innovation solutions."

The Personal Nature of Dreams

What an amazing series of adventures—for us—all stemming from the dream of living and working internationally. Traveling the world, moving so often, would not be the first choice for many other people. Several of our friends laugh at us and joke that the authorities still haven't caught up with us yet! Many just can't fathom why we wanted to live and work in all these places, when we could have just stayed put in some comfortable town in the United States.

The answer is simple. This was my dream, and subsequently a dream and adventure shared by my wife and family. Our dream could just as easily have been to put down roots and never move—which was my younger brother's reaction to moving around so much as a kid. That was not my dream. What I'm trying to underscore is that no matter what it is, your dream should be *yours*. You must know what your dreams are—I mean, really know what they are.

CHART YOUR COURSE

Now jump back to pages 146 and 147, and complete the exercises labeled "Dreams: Round 4."

At this point, also ask yourself a few key questions. It doesn't matter what stage of life you are in. You may be a student getting ready to launch your life. You may be an entrepreneur trying to figure out how to bring your idea to life or how to take it to the next level. You may be an employee. You may be an employer. You may be mid-career or retired. You may be unemployed or lost. It really doesn't matter, because the principles for unleashing the full potential of this adventure called your life, or your business, are fundamentally the same.

I've laid out a few thought-starter questions in the back of the book to force you to be honest with yourself. Now, for each dream, write down a few ways that you can get more specific. What do you need to do by when to increase the chances of your bringing each dream to life?

If the work you are doing now, or the company you are working for now, has nothing to do with your most important dreams—what are you doing? What actions are you going to take to align what you are doing with what's most important to you?

CHAPTER 3

Climb Your Ladder of Intentionality

A dream alone, no matter how specific it is, by no means guarantees that you will make it happen. If we were building a sailboat, think of the dream as the hull. It's absolutely critical for a boat, of course, but without anything else, it's woefully insufficient as a vessel to take you where you want to go. It's a critical starting point—but that's all it is. You have to equip the boat to be able to move forward—so let's start equipping it!

What logically follows the definition of your specific dream is for you to get highly intentional about it. Just like the specificity of your dreams, this has to start with an honest assessment of where you stand today. How is what you are doing today getting you closer to achieving your most important dreams? If the answer is *not at all*, then you have a choice to make. You either change what you are doing or you change your dream. It's binary and is the clearest test of how intentional you are about realizing your dreams.

In a volcanic cave on the island of Lanzarote, in the Canary Islands, a bunch of us, sailors who pretended to be able to either sing or play guitar, decided to put on a concert for anyone who wanted to listen. We named our band Accidental Jibe—and this was to be a "one night only" performance. Surprisingly, we actually had a pretty decent crowd. One of our best numbers was a song written by Glenn Marsden in 1987, at a time when he and some of his friends belonged to the Newport Beach Yacht Club—ironically, a place notorious for very light wind. The lyrics of the song are hilarious—at least for a sailor—but they are also very insightful and offer a powerful lesson in intentionality.

The chorus talks about how he and his friends love to sit around the yacht club bar and talk about the things they are going to do. They prefer to do this because then they don't have to contend with big swells out at sea or high winds. The yacht club, of course, doesn't move. It's **safe**! Glenn goes on to brag about his big, fast boat that can win all the races. He sings about going out to sea one day when things went haywire: The halyard broke, and the boom fell down; the main "took off like a bird," and he calls "Mayday" as he dives beneath his berth. He doesn't go out anymore because of that scare and concludes the song by urging his listeners to "be like me and drink to the sea—and don't untie your boat!"

So many of us are metaphorically doing the same thing—sitting around the yacht club bar (whatever that is for each of us), talking about the things we're going to do—either in our careers or in our personal lives. Yet, for fear that something may go wrong, or because of a lack of intentionality, many of us simply don't untie our boats.

Levels of Intentionality

There are many ways to describe levels of intentionality. The contemporary philosopher John Crosby proposed the one I like best, which is called the *ladder of intentionality*—and it is totally applicable here. Think of a ladder. Typically, the higher you go on a ladder, the scarier it becomes. The same applies to your level of intentionality.

THINKING ABOUT IT

If you are on the lowest rung of the ladder, you are very safe, but your level of intentionality is low. Here, you are merely thinking about something. You can have the thought, but you don't share it with anyone, so the idea can enter your mind and leave just as easily without anyone knowing.

When I was younger, I thought I might like to be a rock star. (What teenage boy doesn't share that dream?) It wasn't a serious desire, and I didn't tell anyone. I also didn't act on it. I could sing pretty well, but I didn't learn to play an instrument well, I didn't form a band, and I didn't write any songs. I had a dream that was not specific at all, and

I really had no intention of ever making it happen. As I grew up, the dream simply faded away. I did not embark upon the adventure, and there was no accountability; I had not taken any risk and certainly had not taken any action. Stick to this rung on the ladder, and your chances of unleashing your full potential are low.

WRITING IT DOWN

The next rung on the ladder increases your level of intentionality quite a bit. You've climbed a little higher. This rung typically involves writing something down—much like I hope you have been doing in the back of this book. This is certainly better than just thinking about something, because there is a risk that someone else could see it and hold you accountable to it.

By the way, that someone who's holding you accountable can also be you. Once you've written something down, you will reread it and try to hold yourself accountable. Think about it for a second. Why do so many of us write down our "to do" lists? They help us get stuff done. And we take great joy in crossing things off the list! That's holding ourselves accountable. But at the end of the day, while writing down a list is better than just thinking about something, the level of intentionality is still relatively low.

I have sat through many strategic planning sessions at large, multinational companies and have reviewed literally hundreds of business plans. In many instances, I could immediately tell that the level of intentionality for the plan was low. The managers had no intention of actually doing what was written on the paper; the plans were written down simply because the team thought that's what senior management was expecting or wanting to see. By the way—don't ever fall into this trap. It will catch up with you eventually.

There was one senior leader in a company I used to work for who was notorious at this. In working sessions, we would share with him our long-term strategic plan for the next several years. He usually didn't think the agenda was sexy enough or "full" enough for senior management back at headquarters, so he'd add a whole bunch of stuff that we knew was not funded and that he knew wouldn't be funded either, but it "looked good." So when he'd fly to headquarters and present the plan, it had the illusion of being intentional (because it was written down), but it really wasn't. If you are a senior leader, I'd suggest you check to ensure that this culture doesn't exist through the ranks of your company. It's a real sickness that leads to wasted time, lost productivity, lost integrity, and lost respect for the leadership of the organization.

But a low level of intentionality can show up in other places besides business plans. It can appear everywhere, in everything, and in everybody. I have run into an awful lot of people during my career who know they are in the wrong job. They know it, and their managers know it, because more often than not, they are not performing well. The ironic thing is that most of these people stay in the job for fear of losing it and because of the theoretical appeal of advancement, when in reality their "misalignment" makes them more likely to lose their job and less likely to advance. They are stuck and often feel like a victim, as though somehow their lack of advancement is the company's fault.

I remember very clearly an assistant brand manager who was working for me when I arrived in the United Kingdom. We'll call him Paul. Paul was a good guy—trustworthy, loyal, a hard worker, and someone you could rely on to get stuff done. Everyone liked Paul. He was a good performer but didn't have the leadership skills that P&G required of their brand managers.

And everyone before me had just passed the buck. They didn't fire him (because he hadn't done anything wrong), but they were also not honest with him about the fact that he was never going to be promoted. Inheriting this issue, I sat down with Paul, and we started a genuine dialog about his dreams. It turns out that his **real** dream was to be in the food business and, ultimately, to own and run his own restaurant and inn. What he was doing in the Fine Fragrances division had absolutely nothing to do with achieving his dream.

Paul was a clear case of low intentionality in action (on both his part and the company's). Once we had clearly and specifically articulated his dream, his level of intentionality skyrocketed. I gave him three months to aggressively look for and land a job in the food-and-beverage industry. He secured a job with a director title at a medium-sized beverage company and was able to resign from P&G with his head held high and his self-esteem intact—as he went off to work in an industry that would help him achieve his dream. What a transformation.

As a side note, it may sound odd, but one of the accomplishments that I am most proud of in my career is that I have received thank-you notes from the vast majority of the people I have had to fire—because

I have used what is commonly a horrible process to help them get their lives on the right track and more aligned with their dreams. I still have Paul's note in my files.

DECLARING IT OUT LOUD

Now, the next rung on the ladder of intentionality goes beyond writing to actually declaring your intentions out loud. You're taking a risk in voicing them. If you declare something out loud, your level of intentionality has gone up significantly. It's your word, and with it comes a sense of responsibility to do what you say you are going to do. At the beginning of the year, millions of people declare that they are going to get fit, lose weight, eat better, go to the gym, save more, or spend less. However, by the end of January, statistics tell us that the vast majority of people have quit. So clearly, for many people, even this level of intentionality is not enough.

STANDING ON THE HIGHEST RUNG

If declaring your dream is not the highest rung on the ladder of intentionality—what is? You are somewhere near the top of the ladder when you have been so effective and energizing in your declaration that you actually get other people talking about it; helping you act on it; and as was the case for us, really supporting you in making your dream happen. As we read at the beginning of the book, Martin Luther King Jr. was brilliant at this.

Get others talking about it

Declare it out loud

Write it down

Think about it

Another example is John F. Kennedy, who was a master. When he declared the dream that, within a decade, the United States would send a man into space, land him on the moon, and bring him safely back to Earth, no one knew how to do it. But JFK was very specific, made a very compelling case, and his level of intentionality and energy was so high that everybody—not just in the United States but across the globe—was talking about it. Talk about an adventure! The project was full of technological and human risk, and yet NASA successfully realized the dream one year ahead of schedule. If JFK had simply written a memo from his desk in the Oval Office, I can guarantee the impact would not have been the same. He rallied a driving force by declaring his dream in such an inspiring way.

Whether you agree with the benefits of dams or not, another powerful example of being on the highest rung on the ladder of intentionality is the Aswan High Dam, which was completed in 1970 in Egypt. Back in 1956, President Nasser of Egypt had a specific dream. He had a dream of an Egypt that could supply all of its own energy needs, thus reducing dependence on foreign oil and all the associated flow of money out of the country. He went so far as to declare that not only could Egypt be energy independent, but it could also sell energy to its neighboring countries—thus lifting the people of the country out of poverty. All they needed to do was build the massive High Dam, using fifty-seven million cubic yards of earth and rock,[9] to harness the power of the Nile in a place called Aswan, and they'd be set. He declared such a specific dream, and declared it with such a powerful level of intentionality and tenacity, that everyone was talking about it, and the dam was built. Today, the Aswan High Dam supplies Egypt with ten billion kilowatt hours of energy per year.[10] Although it has been unable to single-handedly lift the people of Egypt out of poverty, imagine where the country would be today without it.

• • •

9   "This Day in History: July 21, 1970," History.com, accessed March 6, 2016, http://www.history.com/this-day-in-history/aswan-high-dam-completed.

10   "Aswan High Dam," *Encyclopaedia Britannica*, last updated April 9, 2014, http://www.britannica.com/topic/Aswan-High-Dam.

As mentioned earlier, upon returning from our voyage I was appointed chief marketing officer of PepsiCo's International Foods business. But having sailed through so much trash littering our oceans and seeing the islands of the South Pacific awash in plastic containers that had been swept off the US West Coast, over three thousand miles away, a new dream had taken shape. I wanted to do something—anything—to help the environment.

Once I started digging into the data, my commitment to this was strengthened even further. Back in 2009, the American Beverage Association estimated that there are about 650 **billion** beverage containers produced every three years in the United States[11]—a simply staggering number. We are an on-the-go society and want our drinks whenever and wherever we want them. Based on the recycling rates in 2009, over four hundred **billion**[12] of those containers were projected to make it into our landfills, into our waste streams, and into our oceans.

What a crime. We, as a society, know it is important to take care of our planet and recycle, and yet, collectively as a society, we are low on the ladder of intentionality and don't take nearly enough action.

With the support of my boss, Salman Amin, and standing on the highest rung on the ladder of intentionality, we persuaded the company that we needed to embark on a new and different consumer-facing approach to recycling. The **Dream Machine** was born.

We had a very specific dream—to improve the beverage-container recycling rate in the United States from thirty percent to forty percent in three years—and not just through our actions but also by stimulating similar actions from our competitors. Rather than use a traditional (and failed) approach of a big company going it alone, we created a

---

11   Info from an internal company document, fully consistent with Ecocycle.org's environmental facts report, January 1, 2010.

12   Ibid.

new business model that leveraged partners with more knowledge and expertise than us. We partnered with an expert in waste removal and recycling, Waste Management; a rewards-based technology platform called Greenopolis; and a wonderful organization that's the brainchild of Dr. Mike Haynie at Syracuse University, the Entrepreneurship Bootcamp for Veterans with Disabilities (EBV).

So what exactly was the Dream Machine? Physically, it was a recycling kiosk that you could find in front of stores or on college campuses. It was a technologically enabled kiosk that would reward you for depositing any recyclable bottles or cans. And it offered three dreams.

First, it offered the dream of a cleaner planet for our kids and generations to come. Second, it fulfilled the dream of material rewards for those who recycle. Each time you recycled in a Dream Machine, you received zip code–specific discounts on food and entertainment. And third—and perhaps most important—the partnership with EBV enabled ordinary consumers to thank our disabled veterans by helping them realize the dream of starting and sustaining their own business. The more people recycled, the more money was generated to help fund the expansion of the EBV program nationwide.

Despite a very limited operating budget, the Dream Machine's approach was so unique that it received an enormous amount of sustained, positive public relations and press coverage (everyone was talking about it!). As we had hoped, our competition also expanded their recycling programs in response to ours. And within three years, the beverage-container recycling rate in the United States had increased from thirty percent to thirty-six percent—not all the way to our original goal, but massive progress in the right direction. The program has since evolved—as most dreams are prone to do—but I am very proud of the level of intentionality demonstrated by the small team inside PepsiCo and of what we were able to achieve as a result.

Commit to Intentionality

If the first of the big dreams in my LifeBoat was to live and work internationally, the second (which should be obvious to you by now) was to sail around the world. My wife had a dream to travel the world, so we decided that we'd combine the dreams and sail around the world together. After clearly establishing our dream, we knew that we needed to get highly specific about it—and highly intentional about it. We had often talked about the idea in vague generalities with our friends, and of course, it always laid the foundation for lively discussion. But we knew we had to get highly intentional to make sure we didn't just sit around the yacht club bar and talk about the things we were going to do.

There were some clear parameters—just like there are with any project. We wanted to go when the kids were old enough to remember the voyage, old enough for them to be able to help us, and old enough for the adventure to shape both them and us in a meaningful way. And yet, we still wanted them to be young enough that we didn't mess up high school, girlfriends, and boyfriends, and still young enough that it was okay to hang out with Mum and Dad. For those of you with children, you know that's a pretty small window of opportunity. As we worked this through, we knew we needed to do this when the kids were about twelve and ten, so the years had to be 2007 or 2008.

At first, we started declaring our intentions for real to our closer friends and family. It would invariably meet with mixed but highly charged reactions. Many people who heard what we planned to do were on the edge of their seats with excitement. *What kind of boat will you sail? What route will you take? How will you school the kids? What will you do in bad weather?* They were full of questions, but these were the ones we were asking ourselves as well.

Other people (including my parents!) were simply petrified for us and thought we'd gone mad. *Why would you do this? What about work? What*

about safety at sea? How long will you be out of sight of land? Thirty days!!!
Oh my God, you're fools, and you're irresponsible! All their objections and
issues came to life! My parents eventually morphed into supporters
once they understood we were really going to do it and had planned
carefully to do it safely.

There wasn't anyone we discussed the voyage with who didn't have
a strong opinion one way or the other. For us, the more we declared
it, the more excited we got, the more people started talking about it,
and—importantly—the more committed we got to making it actually
happen. Now we weren't just carrying our dreams; we were carrying
the dreams of many others with us. We were on the top rung of the
ladder of intentionality.

I think the biggest test of our intentionality was when I sat down
with my wonderful boss, Pedro Padierna, in Mexico. Not only did I
declare the dream, but I also asked for his help in making it happen. I
was not reckless about this. I sat down with Pedro two years ahead of
our planned departure date. I laid out all the specifics—why we were
doing it, why we needed to do it starting in May 2007, how I loved
the company and didn't want to have to resign—so he could help me
arrange for an extended sabbatical.

I remember his reaction to this day: "One of the things I love most
about my job," he said, "is that I never know what's going to happen on
any given day. This is a first, and I'll figure out a way to help you make
it happen." He didn't know how he was going to do it, but he was fully
committed to helping me—helping us—make it happen.

This was a high-risk move. Pedro could just as easily have taken a
different approach: "Well, Jeremy, that's nice, but we don't do sabbati-
cals here at PepsiCo. Thanks for sharing your dream and your commitment to it. We're now going to figure out a transition plan for you to
leave the company with minimal disruption to the business!" This is not

an unrealistic scenario. Had I still been working at P&G, a sabbatical would not have been an option. Therefore, it was a scenario that Pat and I had planned for financially. If the company decided to fire me, I would just have to find a new job when we returned. Thank goodness that wasn't necessary.

Because we were so intentional about our dream, it became infectious. Our family and friends rallied to help make it happen, and Pedro, as always, was good for his word. He helped convince Mike White, the president of PepsiCo International, and Steve Reinemund, the company's CEO, to support us. We all agreed that my sabbatical would begin in May 2007 and that I would report back to work, somewhere in the world, on September 1, 2008.

JFK was highly intentional, and we got to the moon and back ahead of schedule; Paul became highly intentional and got both his career and life on track; and I was highly intentional about the Dream Machine recycling program and our dream to sail the world, so I made both a reality. If the specific dream is the hull of the sailboat, then a high level of intentionality represents the rigging and the sails—they are the critical components of the sailboat that enable you to make forward progress! Low intentionality is like weak rigging. It will break when pressured, and your forward motion will cease. Don't let that happen to either your business adventures or your life adventures. Build strong rigging that will withstand a lot of pressure, a lot of strong storms, and that will propel you forward.

CHART YOUR COURSE

Now jump to the back of the book again, to pages 148 and 149. By now, I hope that you have generated a long list of dreams—both big and small—across all elements of your LifeBoat. You have prioritized the top five in the boat. You have taken those top five and you have articulated them with great specificity—because the more specific they are, the less you'll focus on the obstacles, fears, and issues that will get in the way of your achieving them. Now, define where you are on the ladder of intentionality with each of those dreams, ranking your intentionality with a score of 1 to 10, where 1 is really low intentionality and 10 is highly intentional.

Here's the next challenge: What are you going to do, **starting tomorrow**, to significantly ramp up your intentionality to make the most important of these dreams come to life? I'd suggest you sit down with the people you love or the people who support you. Declare your specific dream(s) to them first. You may get some pushback and questions, but you know it will be coming from a place of support. Then, as your confidence builds, start telling as many people as you can. The more you talk about it, the more you declare it, the more committed you will become.

Pat and I sat down with our parents first to share our sailing dream. They were less than enthusiastic about the idea but eventually understood and supported us. We then told our close relatives, then our friends, and then our colleagues. With every declaration, our dream, our adventure, became more real, and our resolve to make it happen became stronger.

If you are like many of the clients I work with, you'll be sweating right about now, because fundamentally, this will challenge whether you are serious about your dreams or whether you are just sitting around the yacht club bar talking about the things you're going to do. Being highly intentional about your dreams means you will behave differently tomorrow than you did yesterday. So you'll either be sweating with excitement or with worry!

CHAPTER 4

Ready Yourself, Your Crew, and Your Ship

We've discussed two of the key fundamentals to unleashing your full potential. The first is to *dream specifically* so that you can deal with all the objections, issues, fears, and dreads one by one as they crop up. That's the hull of the boat. The second is to significantly *increase your level of intentionality* to make those specific dreams happen. That's the rigging and the sails that any sailboat needs to harness the wind and propel the boat forward. Not surprisingly, these are important, but not sufficient for you to realize your dreams.

You might well have a dream to be a NASCAR or Formula One race car driver, and you might be highly intentional about that dream, but if you fail to plan and prepare well, we all know that it will end in disaster.

You've been driving an automatic car all your life; how do you shift gears in a car with a manual transmission? How do you accelerate to get the maximum amount of speed in the shortest possible time? How do you brake without killing your momentum? How do you maximize grip through the corners, while not sacrificing speed? How do you speed around the track without skidding off? How do you maximize slipstream? What even is slipstream? How do you read all the information on the steering wheel and relay the information back to your pit crew for them to make adjustments on the fly? How do you raise money for your team? How do you prepare your body for hours of excessive g-forces? You get the idea. If you fail to plan and prepare in this scenario, your race will certainly not end with victory and is likely to end with you in the hospital.

Perhaps one of your dreams is to lose thirty pounds. If you fail to plan and prepare your exercise routine and your diet adequately enough, your progress will be slow, you will lose enthusiasm or commitment, and you'll fail.

If it is self-evident that planning and preparation is so vital to unleashing our full potential, why are we typically so lousy at it for our everyday work lives and our everyday personal lives?

This is a big topic. Because I don't know what your specific dreams and adventures are in your LifeBoat, I am not in a position to give you a "prescription" for what it means to plan and prepare well for you. But I can help you create your own approach by sharing with you some key examples of how others and I have planned and prepared well to realize both our business dreams and our personal dreams. Think about how you could adapt these examples and actions for yourself. This will help equip you with the skills and capabilities you are going to need to harness the hull you have built and the rigging and sails you have installed to actually sail the boat in the direction you want to go.

Ready Yourself

I am standing at a workbench at the Mack Boring Yanmar distributor in New Jersey. "Welcome to Marine Diesel Mechanics," bellows the large and gregarious instructor. "In front of you is the same engine that you have in your boat. It is an expensive engine, and it's fully functioning. Over the next few days, you will be taking the engine apart—learning how to diagnose problems, and learning how to put it all back together. And just so we're clear, I'm not going to let you leave until it runs smoothly again!"

Out on the open ocean, you are your own mechanic, so part of our planning and preparation meant my learning to be a much better mechanic.

Fast-forward to the town of Marseilles in the south of France. *Hakuna Matata*, our brand new catamaran sailboat, sailed in from South Africa after a seven-thousand-mile delivery voyage up the coast of Africa. The delivery captain was quick to point out upon arrival that only one of the two engines was working properly. Time to go to work!

Following my bench training, I started taking parts of the engine off and inspecting them, to troubleshoot the problem. It turns out that the injectors that spray diesel into the engine had fused almost shut and were not spraying uniformly as they should. A typical root cause for this is bad or dirty fuel, but the delivery captain documented that he had filled both engines up at the same location, so that didn't make sense. I took samples of diesel from the starboard (right-side) tank and samples from the port (left-side) tank. They were distinctly different colors! One of the tanks was pure diesel; the other was a mix of diesel and saltwater—a catastrophic combination for the injectors. Perplexed, we then worked on *how* the saltwater was getting in. It turns out that the fuel-tank venting hose had been installed incorrectly at the factory, so rather than venting fumes out, it was funneling saltwater in.

We ordered new injectors, replaced the vent hose using the correct length and positioning, and were on our way. This whole process took weeks and ended up cutting our Mediterranean cruising by quite a bit. But we had planned and prepared well, and we got it fixed.

• • •

How might this same level of planning and preparation help you dramatically accelerate the sales and profit growth of your business? Let's assume you work in or are running a business or project. It could be big, could be really small; it doesn't matter. You want to increase sales by x and profit by y and plan to do all that by z date. When I work with businesses or companies—both large and small—I am constantly amazed by the lack of precision in their objectives—their dreams—as well as the vagueness of their strategies, plans, and actions to achieve them.

To unleash the full potential of any business, the first part of planning and preparing well is to really understand what's going on today. If you own or run an enterprise, do you truly understand your current situation? Here are a few questions you can ask yourself to get a handle on what's going on now:

- What business are you really in? For example, is Virgin in the airline business or the entertainment business? It's impossible to focus on a specific dream if you don't fundamentally understand what business you are in.

- What's the unmet consumer need? Why has that need not been met yet?

- Why are sales and profit flat (or growing or declining)? So many answers to this question are superficial or circular in logic. "Sales are declining because orders to x customer were down." That's not helpful. Why were they down? A demand issue? A supply issue? A quality issue? A lack of competitiveness? What's the root cause? Once you determine the actual cause, you can determine how it affects your business overall.

- What is the strength of your brand, product, or service? Is it both highly distinctive and highly relevant?

- What is the culture of your company? What values are important to you and your company and why? How's the team, and why? Do they work well as a team, or are they simply a collection of individuals? What is their level of talent? How well trained are they to do the job you're asking them to do?

This list is certainly not exhaustive. There are many more questions you should be asking. This is just to give you an idea of how deep you should be digging to really understand what's going on with the consumer or customer, your market, and your competition. The better you understand all these factors, the deeper the insights you will unearth— all of which will help you plan and prepare better, thus giving you an edge and increasing the odds of achieving your business's potential.

So the foundation of real planning and preparation starts with taking the time to ask yourself all the tough questions. To bring the dream to life, you must first answer those questions with brutal honesty. Then use those answers to determine the actions required to address the most important requirements one by one. If you map these out (this is the planning stage), you can move to preparation. We are bombarded by so much data now and so many email messages and such (the small stuff) that they fill up the jar before the big stuff (your knowledge) can find a place. Real planning and real preparation simply don't happen often enough or are not undertaken with enough depth.

The cold, hard fact is that over ninety percent of new businesses and new innovations fail.[13] If people asked more of the right questions up front and answered those questions honestly, I am absolutely convinced that many more would succeed. Again, the better you do this, the clearer the plan will be that you can map out for yourself *and your team* to get the work done so that you'll be well on your way.

Succeeding in business is not usually about being brilliant in setting the vision, the objectives, and the strategies. Ninety percent of it is execution, and for that, you need a team of people who not only understand what it is they are supposed to do (the plan), but who have also been trained well and empowered (prepared) to do it.

• • •

Following sixteen years at Procter & Gamble and ten years at PepsiCo, I embarked on a new adventure at a lighting-technology company. When I walked in the door as CEO of The Lighting Science Group, it was clear that the company had neither planned nor prepared well. Despite having some phenomenal products, the company had no clear vision, no objectives, no strategies, and no aligned plans. It is therefore no surprise that the company had never made money; that it was not keeping pace with market growth (despite being an early innovator in the industry); and that employee morale was a disaster.

Working with thought leaders at all levels of the company, I quickly established and articulated a new vision and mission for the company (the dream) and declared that to our associates, our customers, and our shareholders. I also immediately started asking and getting answers

---

13   Neil Patel, "90% of Startups Fail: Here's What You Need to Know About the 10%," *Forbes*, January 16, 2015, http://www.forbes.com/sites/neilpatel/2015/01/16/90-of-startups-will-fail-heres-what-you-need-to-know-about-the-10/#7e92d37355e1.

to all the kinds of questions I laid out a few pages earlier. Within two months, we had established new objectives, strategies, and plans for the company—secured the approval of the board of directors—and set to work turning the company around.

We created a whole new approach to branding, which was designed to build value for the company and consumers. We focused our innovation pipeline on those innovations that aligned with our branding strategy. We committed to really commercializing those innovations, rather than just inventing stuff that we felt good about but that never made it into consumers' and customers' hands. We began a massive transformation of the supply chain, shifting production from a toxic relationship with an ineffective manufacturer in Mexico to an eager new manufacturing partner in China, where ninety percent of the components for LED lights are made.

The organization had grown too big for the company's level of revenue and the size of the company's losses, so we also had to reduce the size of the company by over half. For the remaining employees, we began to implement performance objectives, appraisals, and tracking for the first time, so they each understood what they were being asked to do and how they would be measured. I thought I was well on the way to unleashing the full potential of the business.

But it turns out I was wrong.

What I had underestimated was the level of distrust within the organization, the level of distrust and dysfunction of the executive team, and the paralysis caused by big disagreements between the various investors in the company. I had not done enough digging on the people and the organization, and it became a big barrier. I failed to plan and prepare well enough in this area so, despite all that progress, I was still unable to unleash the business's full potential.

Ready Your Crew

Back to our sailing adventure. You may have seen those crazy car commercials where the driver is doing something spectacular (often computer generated) and the words scroll across the bottom of your screen: "Professional Driver—Do Not Attempt." Well, in a similar vein, no one should embark on a voyage to sail the world without planning and preparing well. If you do it and survive, put it down to dumb luck and nothing else.

Given the fact that we had never done anything like this before and that we were going with our kids, Pat and I wanted to ensure that we were as well prepared as we could possibly be. How? Safety was of paramount concern to us. The first thing we did was find a group of like-minded sailors who were doing the same thing. We found this in a group called the Blue Water Rally, based out of the United Kingdom. When you join this kind of sailing rally, you pay the team a fee for support throughout your voyage. So we instantly had a team that could help us, could guide us, and we had a network of other boats crossing the ocean at the same time as us.

Although we would not see the other boats while crossing the ocean (boats go at different speeds and take different routes), we knew we could be in radio contact daily and that if we got into serious trouble, other boats would not only know where we were but also could likely get to us in a day or two. This seemed to us like a great safety net.

The Blue Water Rally organizers were also immensely helpful at getting the boats through tricky spots like the Panama Canal (where, if you are on your own, you can end up spending months waiting to go through); at organizing fascinating tours with the boards of tourism in many remote locations; at securing spare parts to replace those that inevitably give up after months of saltwater exposure; and at organizing great parties for everyone to enjoy.

We needed the kids to be able to navigate effectively and to be able to handle the boat in the event that either—or both—of us were incapacitated or killed, so we worked with the Steve Colgate Offshore Sailing School to go through a thorough navigation and boat-handling training for the whole family. Not only did we all train in navigation, but also "Cap'n Willy" went out with us for some real boat-handling training. It's much easier for the kids to learn all this stuff when it's not Dad who's doing all the teaching (see figure 4.1)! I think Elena remains one of the youngest graduates the Offshore Sailing School has had. She was eight.

Figure 4.1. Elena learning boat handling.

As I mentioned at the beginning of this chapter, I took a marine diesel mechanics course to be able to troubleshoot and service either our auxiliary engines or our generator. That turned out to be a really valuable investment.

Pat took an advanced radio communications course so that she had an in-depth knowledge of how to communicate most effectively with our long-range single-sideband radio and how to get the most out of it. She also took a marine medical course, and although she certainly didn't become a certified surgeon, she knew just enough to be dangerous with a skin stapler!

I remember her sitting down with the kids, showing them the stapler, and threatening them in a serious yet somewhat playful tone, "Don't make me use this!"

Pat also participated in abandon-ship training with other Blue Water Rally friends (see figure 4.2). There were a few really critical things she learned in that training. First of all, life rafts are small, cramped, uncomfortable, and wet, so you *really* want to avoid having to use one. If you are in a situation where you need to use one, she learned, you should always step *up* into a life raft from your boat, not *down* into it. Far too many people abandon their boats too early and end up being lost at sea when their boats are ultimately found.

Figure 4.2. Pat learning abandon-ship techniques.

Ready Your Ship

In our case, this was not metaphorical. We had to pick the right boat—a critical factor in any voyage of this kind. Pat has a lousy spine, so we decided that we would sail a catamaran (a boat with two hulls) rather than a monohull. The primary reason is that catamarans sail much flatter than monohull sailboats, which tend to sail heeled over at about fifteen degrees. Leaning to counteract the heel is a strain, especially on long passages, and even more so if you have a bad back. Strain leads to fatigue. Fatigue leads to accidents. Not only would a catamaran be much less of a strain on Pat's back, but also we decided that less fatigue would eliminate many sources of unnecessary family tension throughout the voyage. I don't think it's unique to our family, but we tend to be grumpier when we're tired.

There are several other benefits of a catamaran that we also found attractive. There's the benefit of more space—not unimportant when you have two tweens aboard. Bradley and Elena had their side of the boat; Pat and I had ours (see figures 4.3 and 4.4). There's the benefit of speed. Because catamarans have two hulls, they don't need the heavy lead keel required in a monohull. Without all that lead, they sail faster. There's the benefit that they can't easily be sunk. If you spring a big leak in a monohull, the only thing you can be sure of is that it will soon be sitting upright at the bottom of the ocean! If a catamaran breaks in two, the lack of heavy lead along with the way the compartments are designed enable it to float. We'd all be wet and miserable, but we'd have our boat to cling to on the surface of the ocean rather than watching it sink to the ocean floor.

Figure 4.3. Hakuna Matata *at anchor in the San Blas Islands.*

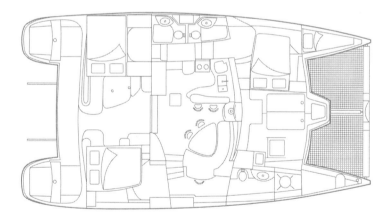

Figure 4.4. The Leopard 43 floor plan.

With the choice of boat design settled, we then had to pick our catamaran (*cat* for short) from among the literally thousands on the market. We chose a forty-three-foot "Leopard 43" catamaran built by Robertson and Caine out of South Africa. These cats are sailed straight out of the boatyard to destinations thousands of miles away. They have an impeccable offshore safety record and, because they sell a version of these boats to the Moorings and Sunsail charter companies, these are among the best-selling catamarans throughout the world. We decided that if the boat needed serious repairs somewhere around the globe, having this brand of boat would increase the likelihood of us finding help and parts.

Another important aspect of planning and preparation was our financials. We knew we would not get paid during our sabbatical (and certainly didn't expect to be), so we began saving our money for the trip four years ahead of actually setting sail. Each month, we'd save more than we were used to saving and put the money in our world-adventure account. As a consequence, we were able to have an income and not worry (at least not too much) about it during the course of our voyage.

A final aspect of preparation that we needed to plan for was the kids' education. We were not sure where we would be posted at the end of the trip, so we decided it was important for the kids to have some sort of documentation that they were homeschooled during the course of the voyage. We investigated all the options and finally settled on a homeschooling program offered by Calvert. We essentially bought fifth and seventh grade "in a box." The program was very self-directed. The kids studied while en route and took tests, which we would fax or send in once we reached port. We were most diligent about English and mathematics—as we did not want them to fall behind their peers in these critical subjects. We were less strict about subjects like geography and history—because we figured the kids were actually living it. This approach enabled them to get full academic credit for the school year.

We dedicated a **huge** amount of effort to planning and preparation to make this particular dream come true, and in the process, we learned a ton—all because it was critical to making this dream, this adventure, a reality.

Planning and Preparation in Action

Shifting gears and going back to my original LifeBoat of dreams/adventures, another one of my top five dreams back in 1987 was exciting but relatively straightforward. I wanted to buy and fix up both a house and a classic car. My dad was always very handy and, thankfully, passed that ability on to his three sons. By teaching us how to fix things and build them ourselves, he actually prepared me well to realize this dream.

For my brothers and me, fixing things is fun. But I had to do my fair share of planning as well. For the house, I wanted to buy a small one, not a big one (not really a problem because I couldn't afford to buy a big one anyway). Just like the previous examples, I had to begin by asking myself as many questions as possible and answering them honestly. How much house could I afford? How much could I afford in renovations? What kind of work did I want to do—cosmetic or structural? How much time could I really dedicate to the project? (I was simultaneously starting my career.) Where should the house be located, and why?

With all my planning and subsequent preparation, I was able to embark on the adventure of homeownership with a fixer-upper just on the edge of the chic Hyde Park neighborhood in Cincinnati. My friends would all joke that I was "Hyde Park adjacent." Given the location, I was able to buy the house for substantially less than I would have had it been quite literally across the street.

It was a thousand-square-foot single-story house that needed a moderate amount of work—mostly cosmetic and mostly just good old sweat equity. I roped my family and friends into helping. Together, we stripped so many layers of wallpaper off the walls that the house actually felt bigger! Fresh coats of paint on the inside as well as on all the exterior trim, shutters, and foundation really transformed the house. Ductwork for forced-air heat was already in place, so I installed a central air-conditioning unit, which not only made the house more comfortable in the summer but also added a lot of value. I also set to work rejuvenating the front and back yards. The whole adventure was a blast and turned out to be a wise financial move. When I sold the house two years later to move to Baltimore, I sold it for thirty percent more than I paid for it, which more than doubled the investment I had made.

The classic-car dream was much the same and, again, was enabled in large part by how Dad taught us to fix things. Planning for this dream was also important. I wanted a car in moderate shape that I could work on, not one in need of a massive rebuild. It needed to be classic, but not an exclusive classic because that would have been too expensive. I had always loved Alfa Romeos, and after several months of scouring the ads (this was before the Internet and all the online car marketplaces that exist today), I found an old Spider convertible in the newspaper that looked interesting. I was hooked the minute I saw the car parked in a cobblestone courtyard under a large oak tree and a cloudless blue sunny sky. She was (and still is) navy blue, with a burgundy red interior—and plenty of rust and bits and pieces that didn't work! Perfect.

I had a lot of fun restoring that car, doing whatever I could by myself but also spending a fair amount of time with experts who really knew what to do.

I don't think I planned the car restoration particularly well. The whole adventure was more of a learning experience. The more work

I did on the car, the more I learned what to do and what not to do. Upon reflection, the Alfa was most likely just preparation for my next car-restoration project.

When we moved internationally, my older brother took possession of the car, and it's still in the family today. He, by the way, has done a much more comprehensive restoration and now participates in classic-car rallies across the Midwest.

Swimming for Gold

Another notable example of planning and preparation in action that has been widely publicized really helps underscore the importance of this concept. I find the quest of Michael Phelps and his coach Bob Bowman to be very inspirational. By any measure, Michael was already a hugely successful athlete, having won six gold medals and two bronze medals in the 2004 Athens Olympics and numerous national and international competitions. However, he knew that he had more potential. Michael had a very specific dream: to become the most decorated Olympian of all time. Period. His specific goal was to achieve this during the 2008 Beijing Olympics. And to do it, he would need to win gold in eight races, ranging from short sprints to long relays, and in all four strokes.

Even with his level of talent, he couldn't just show up at the Olympics and realize his dream. No. He and his coach asked themselves the tough questions about Michael's stamina, speed, and physical and mental strength. With honest answers to these questions, together they planned out a preparation program—Michael's training regimen—that was both long and intense. Michael's challenge was not only to continue building his strength but also to improve his endurance and his straight-line speed. According to Roger Lockridge of Bodybuilding.com, Michael was in the pool six days a week, *and* doing circuit training in the gym three days a week.[14] He had a specific diet designed to enable his body to perform at its best. Once at the Olympics, he had to pace each of his races in such a way that he could peak during the gold-medal races.

As we all know, it paid off, and he realized his dream. You may view that as an extreme example, but I beg to differ. That was his dream; it's certainly not mine, and I doubt it's yours, but it was what he wanted. What we can take away is that he was very specific about it. He had a very high level of intentionality (the whole world was talking about his quest), and he planned and prepared well.

Much in the same way I've described throughout this book, his dream was full of risk. He was explicitly setting expectations of what success should look like—so much so that had he "only" won six races instead of eight, we would likely have viewed that as failure. But dreams and risk typically go hand in hand!

By the way, there's another important thing we can learn about planning and preparation taught by Michael. Think about the LifeBoat again for a moment. I don't think Michael's was very complete. He was completely defined by his swimming and his athletics. Given this, he did not do such a good job of planning and preparing his other Grab Bags for life balance. He ended up in a pretty negative cycle of reckless behavior that threatened his legacy, his relationships, and indeed, his life. Following an intervention by his family and friends, it appears as though he has been able to successfully restore a much healthier balance to his life. How great is that?

---

14   Roger Lockridge, "Phelps the Phenom: What Makes Michael Phelps One of the Best Athletes in History," Bodybuilding.com, last updated July 30, 2012, http://www.bodybuilding.com/fun/michael-phelps-the-phenom.html.

CHART YOUR COURSE

Let's jump to the back of the book again, to page 150. What does planning and preparation look like for your top five? How can you be more intentional and purposeful in this critical area? What do you need to know, to do, and to know how to do before you begin? What equipment will you need? Will you need help from other people, and if so, who?

I have never suggested, and still do not, that realizing your dreams and your full potential is easy. Typically, if it's worth doing, it takes work. And just like delivering breakthrough business results, renovating a house, rebuilding a car, sailing around the world, or going for gold in the Olympics, planning and preparation are absolutely critical. If you are in business, how well are you *really* doing this? The statistical answer is not well enough. This is one of the key reasons that over ninety percent of all businesses fail. It's probably one of the key reasons why so many of our dreams also fail.

CHAPTER 5

Summon Your Courage

The guide is mapping out the day for us as the speedboat shoots across the water at thirty knots. We're en route to a small group of islands on the outer edge of the Galapagos.

"For our first dive," the guide said, "we will be heading down to thirty to forty feet. Visibility isn't all that great today, so let's be sure to stay pretty close together. I need you to keep a close eye on me, and if I give the signal, I want you to calmly make your way to the surface. Make sure to do your safety stop and don't shoot straight up. As you know, that will cause a condition known as *the bends*, where too much oxygen is forced into your bloodstream. Very painful and known to cause death!"

Normally, none of these instructions or reminders would raise my anxiety level. But this time, Bradley—my twelve-year-old son—and I are going diving in rough open water and with hammerhead sharks.

We check all our gear. Buoyancy compensator—check. Weight belt—check. Air pressure—check. We both sit on the edge of the boat, now anchored in the rolling seas between two small islands, place our hands over our masks to keep them in place, and then fall backward into the cold dark blue water with a splash. We descend to thirty feet as instructed. All group members are present and accounted for, with all equipment in order.

And then, in the distance, we spot about twelve sharks, swimming slowly toward us. Elegant, powerful, swift, and magical. We are at once captivated by their presence, excited, and amazed. Not at all frightened. Here we are, sharing the deep blue sea with these magnificent creatures. What a life highlight that I will forever cherish with my son—a life highlight that would never have happened if we had not had the dream to swim with sharks, the intentionality to do it, and the planning and preparation to dive safely. But the adventure would also not have happened if we had not summoned the courage to splash over the side of the boat and dive into the water.

Incidentally, there are probably many of you who think this was just stupid! That's okay. It was our dream—not yours!

> "To dream anything that you want to dream, that is the beauty
> of the human mind. To do anything that you want to do,
> that is the strength of the human will. To trust
> yourself to test your limits, that is the courage to succeed."
>
> —Bernard Edmonds

Courage is a tremendous word, full of depth and meaning. It manifests itself in many different ways, but the **act** of courage is often an outcome of winning the battle in our minds. Courage means overcoming the fears, dreads, and obstacles that prevent us from unleashing our full potential. Here again, I don't know what the dreams are in your LifeBoat, so I can't know the amount of courage or the kind of courage you will need to realize them. Reflecting back on our shipbuilding metaphor again for a moment, your specific dream is the hull of the boat. Your intentionality is the rigging and the sails. Your planning and preparation are the training to be able to sail and navigate the boat. Courage is the wind—the wind that you harness to propel the boat forward! Sometimes only a little wind is necessary. Other times, you need a lot! Here are some perspectives on courage for you to reflect upon.

Set Sail

All glory comes from daring to begin! You are destined to die full of potential if you do not have the courage to metaphorically untie your boat and set sail. Much like your dreams, a boat is perfectly happy to sit at the dock. You can get on, get a slim taste of the dream of setting sail, have a cocktail, and get off—back to your "real" life.

Similarly, your dreams can stay just that; they can be a place in your mind that you visit from time to time. They can live and die there. If that is your choice, that's obviously okay by me. Just please don't adopt a victim mentality as you march through life muttering: *I would have, should have, could have, if only* . . . I strongly urge you to pluck up the courage and take the action required to realize your dreams. You only live once, right? Make it count! How many times have you heard the expression "Live each day as though it were your last"? Are you really doing that?

The real setting-sail date for our seafaring adventure was not the date we actually untied the boat from the dock in Marseilles, France. It was the day I summoned the courage to sit down with Pedro, tell him of our dream, and ask for his help to make it happen. That's when the cat was really out of the bag. I had to build up enough courage to sit down with my boss and risk losing my job. (As mentioned earlier, we had planned and prepared for that to be an outcome but were sincerely hoping it would not come to that.)

But we're talking about all the dreams in the LifeBoat here, not just one. In the work Grab Bag, I have summoned the courage to set sail throughout the course of my career, and I encourage you to do the same. When I was offered a position at Procter & Gamble Venezuela, we had no real knowledge of the country. We decided to visit and meet the management team; look at some housing and school options; explore Caracas; and get a more close-up feel for the place. At the end of that week, Pat and I reviewed what we had learned. The people working at P&G there were great. The job opportunity/challenge sounded great. Caracas was beautiful. The weather was beautiful year round. Violent crime was very high—mostly as a result of extraordinarily high levels of poverty. There were bullet holes in the elevator—reminders of the attempted overthrow of the government in 1992. And we knew no one! We had the courage to say **yes** and set sail on this adventure, despite our concerns for what might lie in store. That decision opened the door to almost fourteen years of adventure for us throughout Latin America, which filled up many of the other essentials in my LifeBoat—family, friends, philanthropy, finances, and spirit.

After sixteen years, I had the courage to set sail from Procter & Gamble when, as mentioned earlier, I felt I was suffocating in the big bureaucracy of the company's headquarters—a shock after so many years working in a much more nimble international environment. I had the courage to set sail from Schering-Plough within less than a year—when for reasons completely beyond my control, the job I accepted morphed into something completely different and much less attractive. I had the courage to accept a position at PepsiCo in a subsidiary where English was not the primary language of business. It's one thing to be able to converse in Spanish. Running a business in Spanish is a completely different challenge. I had the courage to set sail from PepsiCo when I felt stagnant and, once again, stifled by slow decision-making and bureaucracy. I had the courage to take a job as CEO of a company in a completely different industry and in need of a massive turnaround. When, after much hard work, blood, sweat, and tears, I had an irreconcilable disagreement on the direction of the company with the primary investor in the business, I had the courage to leave. And then I had the courage to set sail again on another adventure—starting my own company.

What's the point here? Certainly not that I have had a host of adventurous career experiences but, rather, that I have always somehow summoned the courage to set sail and to make a change when I've either known or felt the time was right. I have not simply been a victim of "the system" or that vague pronoun "them." I have not stuck around simply because it's the safe thing to do or because of the amount of unvested stock options in my account that I would lose. I've made changes—many of them requiring a fair amount of courage—when my work or situations no longer fit with the dreams in my LifeBoat.

Let's think about your work for a minute, and the line of work you are in doesn't matter. Any meaningful new product, new process, new service, operational approach, requires courage to set sail. After all, as is often said in business, "All ideas are stupid before they're spectacular." You will encounter resistance. Where, in your day-to-day life, can you practice the courage to set sail?

Venture into the Unknown

Back to sailing. It is one thing to set sail; it is an entirely different thing to venture out into the unknown. When we set out from the Canary Islands to sail across the Atlantic—over three thousand miles of open ocean—I think it's fair to say that we were rather terrified. Despite our high degree of intentionality and despite all the planning and preparation I shared earlier, it was still a daunting challenge. Here we were, in this forty-three-foot boat, heading out across a vast sea. We went through all our final safety checks, systems checks, food checks, engine checks, route planning, and so on. Then, in November 2007, after five months exploring the countries lining the shores of the Mediterranean Sea, we hoisted our sails and summoned the courage to set out across an incredible expanse of water—full of unknowns.

Our passage from the Canary Islands, off the northwest coast of Africa, to Antigua in the Caribbean turned out to be amazing in every sense of the word. We quickly settled into a routine, and you'd be surprised how busy you can keep when it seems like there'd be nothing to do.

We developed a simple watch schedule for the nights, to ensure that someone was always up to scan the horizon for other boats, obstacles, or a change in the weather. In good weather, Bradley and Elena would spend several hours a day doing schoolwork. Pat kept busy preparing meals for the crew—keeping us all well fed and full of energy. I would check the engines, rigging, navigation, and a long list of other items on a daily basis to ensure that nothing was going to fail us en route.

At 10 a.m. every day, we would have a Rally roll call using our single-sideband radios to find out what was going on with the other boats making the same journey. Where were they? What kind of weather were they having? How was the crew doing? This routine was occasionally interrupted by a large fish taking the bait that was trolling behind us. We'd have to drop the sails and haul it in. Bradley would crank some hard-rock song on the stereo that had to do with killing. Then we'd kill, fillet, and vacuum-pack the fish to keep us supplied with fresh meat.

In our downtime, we'd read, play guitar, enjoy board games, and often just relax and soak in the seemingly endless expanse of the sea. Elena's favorite spot was on the trampoline mesh stretched between the bows of the boat. From there, she could watch the waves race by under the boat or the clouds race through the sky. We encountered the occasional storm or the occasional flat calm—nothing our planning and preparation couldn't handle.

On one night in particular, there was no wind, and the sea was flat calm. We had one engine on at low revs to keep us moving toward the Caribbean. There was not a cloud in the sky, so the millions of stars were perfectly reflected in the ocean. It literally felt as though we were gliding through space, with stars above us and stars below us. Dolphins, whales, or sharks would join us from time to time. At one point, we came across a pod of baby killer whales so young that their bellies were still pink. Just amazing!

Another highlight was seeing how much the kids were growing as people. One hot day, when there was absolutely no wind, Elena plucked up the courage to go swimming. In the middle of the Atlantic, with a mile or two of ocean beneath her, she jumped off the boat for a swim. How amazing!

After twenty-one days at sea, we made landfall in Jolly Harbour, Antigua. Our first major crossing was an experience like no other, and it would have never happened had we not taken the risk and had the courage not only to set sail but also to venture out into the unknown. In spring 2008, after four months sailing through the islands of the Caribbean; along the north coast of Latin America; through the San Blas Islands; through the Panama Canal; and then through the Galapagos, it was time for us to embark on an even longer passage, over what many consider a more challenging ocean—the Pacific. The amazing thing was that we weren't at all terrified when we set sail four months later. The difference is that we had conquered the Atlantic. We had ventured out into the unknown, and so we knew we could do it (figure 5.1).

Figure 5.1. Two sunsets. We were scared to death when we took the picture on the left, because it was the first night of our first ocean crossing (the Atlantic). We were calm and excited for the picture on the right, the first night of our Pacific crossing. Why? Because we knew we could do it!

So how about you? Typically, it's probably very easy for you to take your dreams and metaphorically go for a quick sail around the harbor. I urge you to practice summoning the courage to venture into the unknown. Start with the smaller stuff in your LifeBoat and build your courage gradually. It's scary at first and full of risk, but the more you practice, the better you'll get, and you'll be well on your way to realizing your dreams.

Keep Going in the Face of Adversity

We've established that taking the steps necessary to realize your full potential is not easy. There is no doubt that you will face all sorts of adversity along the way. I have experienced this in both my professional life and my personal life.

I worked for PepsiCo for ten years. During my fifth year there, Indra Nooyi was appointed CEO of the company. Indra's vision for the company, driven in large part by the external health and wellness pressures facing the company because of the global obesity epidemic, was compelling. She declared, with high intentionality, that PepsiCo would transform its portfolio and improve the health profile of its existing beverages and snacks, while also offering consumers healthier snack and beverage alternatives.

This was a really powerful dream and a *very* challenging one to accomplish. Consumers still love the taste of full-sugar drinks and traditional salty snacks. Transforming the portfolio requires a huge investment of money, time, and resources. The ingredients used are typically more expensive—all of which puts pressure on the company's profit, which Wall Street doesn't like.

The transformation faced a lot of adversity and opposition and many challenges. The journey for PepsiCo is still far from complete, but the biggest mistake the company could ever make is to reverse course. It might be the path of least resistance, but it would spell disaster for the company in the long term and could potentially mean the demise of a company which, despite its success, is still full of potential.

Procter & Gamble had the need to radically transform the company back in the late 1990s. As has been well documented, that is when the company had the courage to decide, in earnest, to operate as a truly global company. Management at the time were clear and decisive: They announced the new direction of the company. Simultaneously, they understood that not everyone would be in agreement with the decision or the new structure. Expressing this concept in a straightforward way to all employees, they urged those people to step forward and take a generous package to leave the company—and, essentially, get out of the way. Despite this level of courage and clarity, it still took the company about five years to make the transition, both operationally and culturally. But they are much stronger today as a result. Imagine the chaos had they not had the courage to keep going in the face of adversity and turned back midway through the journey.

While at P&G, I was challenged to help the team in Argentina accelerate the growth of one of the company's flagship shampoo and conditioner brands. After plenty of planning and preparation, we recommended that the company embark on a massive sampling campaign so that women across the country could experience the superiority of our brand for themselves.

To break through the clutter, we first sent women a mock love letter from a secret admirer describing her hair in beautiful detail. This "letter" was clearly a commercially printed piece, and the text at the end of the letter notified the reader that we would be sending her a sample of the shampoo and conditioner the following week. It never occurred to us that anyone would think this was a real love letter. But after the first wave of letters went out, a few men did, and they hurt their wives. I was mortified. We had the courage to suspend the program immediately, despite the cost. We urgently printed a clarification letter that we sent out to women who had received the first letter. We then rapidly retooled the sampling program to ensure that there was no risk of anyone getting hurt.

Looking at this experience, we had the courage to recommend and invest behind a massive sampling campaign. We had the courage to suspend the program (at great cost) when we found out that a few jealous and ignorant men had hurt their wives as a result. We had the courage not to walk away from sampling altogether, because it was the right thing to do for the business. We changed the approach. We had the courage to keep going in the face of adversity.

• • •

As I mentioned earlier, as we were sailing between New Caledonia and Australia, we got caught in a massive tropical storm that got much bigger than had originally been forecast and that had stalled over the South Pacific. We were in forty- to sixty-mile-an-hour winds and forty-foot waves for three days straight. From time to time, the boat would be completely submerged by errant waves crashing over the boat's side. Almost every corner of the boat was wet, including, of course, the crew. With such big waves and heavy rainfall, the radar could not work. Night was a complete blackout, so we were screaming along, up and down massive waves, with no way to see what was about to hit us or, for that matter, what we were about to hit. We made it safely through that ordeal—the most trying of our voyage. We had to adjust the sails, had to change course, and had to modify our plan. The worst possible thing we could have done would have been to turn back, retrench, and head back into the waves. That would have spelled disaster for the boat—and most likely death for the crew.

I am not for a minute suggesting that you barrel blindly on, and of course, there will always be an exception to this guidance. What I am suggesting, though, is that, based on my experience, more often than not the risk of turning back poses a greater risk to your achievements than having the courage to keep going in the face of adversity. What are some of the smaller storms you are facing in your business or personal life that you can use for practice? How often have you found yourself turning back when the going gets tough or when you have faced adversity? Practice with smaller challenges, and you will find yourself much better equipped to handle the big adversity when it comes your way. The courage to simply keep going in the face of adversity can pull you through and keep you on course.

Ask for Help, and Give It

I'm not sure what happens to us as we age, because it's not as though we're taught specifically *not* to ask for help as adults, but it is amazingly consistent how infrequently we do it. As children, one of the primary ways for us to learn is to ask questions and to ask for help. According to research conducted in 2013, nine-year-old boys ask an average of 144 questions per **day**.[15] And most of us, as we grow up, are eager to help out.

Yet as adults, perhaps especially in the United States, we seem to be embarrassed to ask questions or ask for help because it sends a signal that we can't figure stuff out on our own. In all honesty, I can't think of too many people who have succeeded in this world and unleashed their full potential without help. As always, I am sure there are exceptions, but I think the number is very low.

One beautiful evening, we were sailing into a dangerous anchorage in the San Blas Islands, just off the coast of Panama. The approach is perilous because coral surrounds the vast majority of it, with only a narrow entrance for boats to navigate before safely entering the lagoon. It is best to approach these kinds of anchorages when the sun is high in the sky. This gives you the best chance of seeing the dangers lurking beneath the surface. We timed our arrival badly and were approaching the anchorage later than we should have. The sun was not directly overhead, so although the kids were on the lookout at each bow, we ran aground.

Not good. One of the benefits of a catamaran is that the two hulls make them very stable at sea. Unfortunately, this same feature turns

---

15   "Littlewoods Retailer Survey Finds Mothers Asked 228 Questions a Day," News.com.au, March 29, 2013, http://www.news.com.au/lifestyle/parenting/littlewoods-retailer-survey-finds-mothers-asked-228-questions-a-day/story-fnet085v-1226609073893.

into a liability when you run aground. The boat is *very* comfortable sitting on the ground, and you can't rock it back and forth to break free from the bottom like you can with a monohull. On the East Coast, where we currently sail, you can count on the tides to lift the boat off the bottom if you've run aground. That's not the case in the San Blas, where there is next to no tide.

The first thing we did was not panic. The second thing we did was send the kids off in the dinghy, into the anchorage, to ask for help. There were two boats from Sweden sitting peacefully at anchor. Their skippers were relaxing with cocktails in hand when they were rudely interrupted.

"We have run aground coming into the anchorage!" one of the kids explained when they landed the dinghy. "Can you please help us before it gets too dark?"

There was no "That's not our job," "Sorry, we're in the middle of cocktails," or "That's your problem." They dropped everything and headed over to help us. My rusty Swedish came in handy as they helped us free *Hakuna Matata* from the grips of the coral. It took several hours, and by the time we were free, it was dark. Yet, our newfound Swedish friends then led us carefully through the entrance of the anchorage to ensure that we made it through safe and sound.

• • •

As CEO of Lighting Science, I was fortunate enough to have the former CEO of Philips Lighting USA (and current CEO of TCP Lighting), a Dutch gentleman named Kaj den Daas, on my board of directors. We were in a real hurry to get a strategy in place, but I also wanted it to be at least eighty percent right. I didn't want us to be paralyzed by perfection but wanted our plan to be right enough to work. Rather than stumble along with an inadequate level of knowledge, I invited Kaj to the company for a two-day working session with the leadership team to help us with our strategic plan development.

Our most urgent dream was to turn the company into a profitable enterprise after thirteen years of losses. At a high level, we developed four strategic imperatives to achieve this. First, we wanted to create an added-value brand for the company (in addition to the base business, which supplies a large retailer with the product for their brand). This new brand would offer unique benefits, would be able to command a price premium at retail, and would therefore be profitable. The second strategy was to eliminate a lot of unfocused innovation work and to focus on developing and commercializing a short list of innovations for both the base business and the new brand. The third strategy was to transform the manufacturing infrastructure and to move production to the source of the components. The fourth was to transform the effectiveness, efficiency, and size of the organization.

I didn't ask Kaj to approve the strategies. I actually asked him to "punch as many holes" in them as possible, so that we could strengthen or change them as needed. Was our data accurate? Did our assumptions make sense? What other key insights were we missing? He offered his help and his thirty-plus years of lighting experience to us unconditionally—and was an enormous help. As CEO of the company, I had the courage to ask the questions and ask for help, and he had the courage to help. As a result, we developed a strong set of competitively advantaged strategies on an accelerated schedule. We presented the plan to the board of directors in the first week of March. We secured their agreement, and the very next day, we held an all-company meeting to share the new strategic plan. The following day—we began to execute it.

There are obviously a lot of parallels here for the way we conduct ourselves in our personal affairs and in our business affairs. How often do we have the courage to ask for help—not just in emergencies but also day to day? And just as importantly, how often do we have the courage to give help unconditionally, not expecting anything in return? This is an essential ingredient of the courage I am proposing, because, as I mentioned earlier, most of us need help from others to realize our full potential. You practice it all the time with your kids (if you have any). Now try practicing it more in all the other essentials in your LifeBoat.

Be Humble

It sounds a bit silly to think that you need courage to be humble, but again, I believe it's another critical ingredient in the journey to realize your dreams and adventures and to unleash your full potential. Quite simply, if you are humble, you are typically more self-aware and therefore have the capacity to learn! If you are arrogant, you believe you have all the answers, which blocks your ability to learn. A big part of defining your dreams and adventures, a big part of increasing your intentionality, and a huge part of planning and preparing well will require that you have the ability to learn.

After having failed to make a working lightbulb until he had made something like ten thousand attempts, Thomas Edison supposedly declared, "I did not fail. I just found ten thousand ways that won't work."

It's a very different and transformative point of view—to see your mistakes and failures as part of the process—that enables you to advance your knowledge. Edison was constantly learning, and that led to a "mankind-transforming" breakthrough.

I think Elon Musk is actually a modern-day equivalent—even though outwardly he does not come across as humble. One of his dreams is clean transportation that requires significantly less natural resources, and that doesn't emit the toxic gas that screws up our health and our atmosphere. He didn't just dream up the current Tesla line of vehicles, which are so highly rated that the famed consumer magazine *Consumer Reports* had to revise their ratings system because the car is so excellent on every dimension. He started with a low-production, overpriced two-door Lotus. He ripped out all the guts and transformed it into an electric vehicle. He learned and stumbled along the way. And got better. That learning, coupled with his brilliant business mind and adventurous spirit, helped shape the product he has today.

The humbler we are, the more we learn and the better we can become. This is why—no matter what line of work you are in, or where you are in your life—you should push yourself to experiment more, and you should view failure as a learning tool, not as an enemy.

• • •

While we were in the San Blas Islands, a wonderful Kuna Indian fisherman named Leon befriended us. He first approached us in his sailing skiff with a colorful patchwork sail made of burlap and sheets. We bought some fresh lobster from him and struck up a conversation in Spanish.

"How long do you expect to be here?" he asked.

We didn't respond with the typical "just a few days." Instead, we responded with "As long as it takes for us to learn a bit about these islands and the Kuna Indians."

That immediately opened the door. The following day, we were invited to his village. Leon and his family had nothing, but we were welcomed with open arms and invited to sit around the fire for a drink. We met his wife and four daughters, who ranged in age from ten to eighteen years old. Their "kitchen" was a separate hut with an open fire pit for the cooking. After meeting the family, we toured the village— the school, the medical center, the street (where we joined in a game of street soccer), and the dock.

The following day was a real privilege. We hiked into the foothills lining the coast of Panama, up to the most sacred place for the Kuna Indians—their cemetery. Situated with a breathtaking panoramic view of the San Blas Islands, this is where their dead come to spend eternity. We learned that, rather than being put in a box, the body is laid in a hammock underground, which is then covered with earth. The body is able to swing and relax in a hammock overlooking a spectacular vista for all eternity. How marvelous! When infants die, they are laid in the same hammock as a previously deceased relative. If infants die at six months old or younger, they are considered too young to be separated from their mothers, so they are buried under their mother's hammock, in her home in the village.

What did we learn? Besides all the amazing traditions and day-to-day lives of the Kuna Indians, we learned that being humble opens doors to learning.

. . .

Most of us work for someone else. When our leaders are humble, they harness the power of their organizations rather than demoralizing their employees by making them feel inferior. When leaders demonstrate the importance of being humble and are open to learning, they send that message to everyone. And not surprisingly, organizations that make learning an integral part of their culture are often more successful than those that do not. I have worked for both kinds of bosses, and *far* prefer the former.

If, as you are reading this, you are in a position of authority, what kind of boss are you? Do you have the courage to be humble? It's another essential ingredient that's needed to transform the humdrum of the daily grind into real adventure and to lead you to the realization of your full potential!

Trust Yourself and Your Team

The world can be a funny place at times. We are bombarded with so many negative messages that it's increasingly difficult to know who we can trust. Surveys around the world suggest that people no longer trust their governments. Trust in large corporations is at an all-time low. Trust in banks is even worse—and that's where we keep our hard-earned money! Trust in religion is struggling, because so much evil is done in the name of God. We are bombarded with messages that we cannot trust ourselves to eat properly, that we can't be trusted to manage our money or raise our kids properly—you name it. So why on earth—actually, *how* on earth—can we have the courage to trust ourselves and the teams that support us, whether they are colleagues, family, or friends? Quite frankly, we *have* to, because the alternative is a rather bleak, lonely, unhappy, and much less productive life.

How can you go about building trust in yourself? I believe it is much easier when you have specific dreams, when you are intentional about them, and when you are on the journey of planning and preparing for them to come to fruition. This helps keep you squarely centered on where you are today, where you are trying to go, and what you're trying to do to get there! In my experience, the higher your level of intentionality and the more prepared you are, the more able you are to summon the courage to trust yourself.

When I proposed to PepsiCo that I take a sabbatical to sail the world, I was so focused on that adventure, so intentional, and so prepared that I was able to trust myself—and just do it. Similarly, in business, the clearer you are about what it is that you are trying to accomplish, the more highly intentional you are, and the better you have planned and prepared, the more apt you are to trust yourself. You will be challenged all along the way. And as I have repeated throughout this book, you will make mistakes. You may wander off track—and you can find plenty of learning and potential adventure there—but, fundamentally, you will still have to have the courage to trust yourself.

I have found that the workplace can be full of mistrust, and unfortunately, so can many families and other relationships outside the office. So how can you trust your team? At the office, you really must start with being able to trust yourself. If you are always second-guessing yourself, are not well prepared, and lack the authority that goes along with your responsibility, then trusting yourself will be difficult. Your lack of trust in yourself will be evident to others, and they, in turn, will have a hard time trusting you. The best way I have found to build this trust is to build your knowledge and expertise to the point where everyone knows you are an expert—including you.

But this goes well beyond knowledge or mastery of any given subject. Are you demonstrating behaviors that build trust in yourself and others' trust in you? If you are a gossip, people will be less likely to trust you with confidential information. If you are arrogant and self-centered, people will be less likely to trust that you care about them or their work, because all the signals you are sending are that you are more important than they are. You will never be able to trust your team if you always have the answer (or at least think you do); always have all the ideas; are controlling; and think if a job is worth doing, you might as well do it yourself. This type of behavior is very unproductive, self-limiting for all but a few geniuses, and—frankly—exhausting.

I worked for a gentleman at PepsiCo who was like this. He pretended to listen, but ultimately, his behavior signaled that he didn't trust any member of the team around him, and all good ideas had to come from him. When he was wrong, he'd blame his team, and when his team was right, he'd take all the credit. It created an extremely negative environment; there was no trust, resignations were rampant, and, not surprisingly, the business results were awful.

When this happens at the office, it's typically pretty miserable, and you may be pushed to the point where you summon the courage to move on. However, it can be far more challenging when we lose trust in our family relationships and friendships. I am not going to expand this book with chapters on how to address the many relationship issues and challenges, but I will offer a few simple reflections.

My first reflection is that we all claim that trust has to be earned, and once it is lost, it is almost impossible to rebuild. And yet, every time we get behind the wheel of a car, we are instantly trusting thousands of strangers with our lives—without a moment's thought. We trust that all the other drivers on the road know how to drive, that they know how to follow the rules, and that they won't crash into us. When there is an accident, very few of us stop driving altogether. We get the car fixed, heal any injuries, and then get right back on the road again and trust thousands more strangers. Why, therefore, do we put up so many barriers to trusting ourselves or those closest to us? Think about it!

My second reflection on this is that perhaps we feel the risk of trusting is too great, because often in order to trust, we need to first be vulnerable. Of course! But any important action requires risk, and you must have the courage to take that risk.

Pat and I have many dreams for our lives together. Knowing those dreams, being intentional about them, and planning and preparing for them to come to life together has formed a foundation for us that has no place for mistrust. As we set off sailing the world, all the preparation we had done enabled us to trust our little team. I trusted Pat, Bradley, and Elena with any task, and in turn, they trusted me, so mutiny was avoided!

Without pretending to offer shallow solutions, my only challenge to you is this: Are you being courageous in your trust for yourself and for the trust you have in your family? Practice, practice, practice. The more you practice, the better you'll get.

Be Optimistic

There was another family who set sail around the world several years prior to us. They sailed essentially the same route, and they sailed in a catamaran about the same size as ours. This was a family of six, with children ranging from five to fourteen years old when they set sail. They had been having some issues with getting along with one another and bonding, and so, being the optimists that they were, they decided to set sail around the world! Tension on the boat was apparently high at times, especially between John, the father, and his eldest son, Ben, who apparently didn't want to be there. The father and son had quite a history of disagreements before and during the trip.

In the South Pacific, they shipwrecked on the reef of a remote island. The waves were rough and were literally tearing the boat apart. Then real disaster struck when the mast fell down, pinning John's leg to the boat.

John's leg was gashed badly, he was bleeding out, and the mast simply would not budge. Ben developed a plan—summoning all the knowledge he had gained in Boy Scouts. He fashioned a tourniquet to slow the draining of his father's blood. He led his brother and sisters to safety, carrying them from the wreck to shore. He quickly returned to the boat, where he found his dad on the brink of death, saying good-bye to his mom. He struggled mightily to free the life raft from the twisted wreckage, in order to ferry his dad to shore. He tried one more time, with his mom, to lift the mast and free his dad.

Just then, a big wave hit, with enough force to enable them to lift the mast just enough to free John. They wrapped the leg some more, lifted their very weak captain into the life raft, and got him to shore. They had already radioed for help, found some natives who had a phone, and phoned in to accelerate the helicopter rescue from Tahiti. John lost his leg but kept his life.

If you read their book, you cannot be anything but impressed by their amazing optimism. The trip certainly didn't turn out the way they had planned, but it did achieve the objective of bringing the family closer together. Ben saved everyone's life. Together, they survived a horrific ordeal and had a life experience that brought them closer together than they could have ever imagined.

From John's optimistic viewpoint, losing his leg almost seems like a small price to have paid. For those of you more interested in that story, I'd recommend you read their book—*Black Wave* by John and Jean Silverwood (New York: Random House, 2008). I suspect that many of us would tell a different account of this kind of experience. Catastrophe, tragedy, calamity—all negative sentiments that drive us into a negative, pessimistic frame of mind. We therefore don't learn or move on from the experience. We allow it to define us, and with that, we let it limit our potential and our ability to realize our dreams and future adventures.

Many of you reading this will have had bad experiences that don't have a happy ending. I'm not being glib or suggesting for a minute that you don't mourn the loss of life, violent acts against you, the loss of a job, divorce, tragedies, or other traumatic events. What I am suggesting is that the more courage you have to face both the past and the future with optimism, rather than allowing the experience to drive you to face the future with pessimism, the more you will unleash your full potential throughout the balance of your life.

Christopher Reeve was in the prime of his health, and his acting career was literally flying (he was Superman in *Superman* I–IV [1978–1987], for those of you too young to know!), when he fell headfirst off his horse and broke his neck. Yes, he struggled mightily and, on more than one occasion, wanted to give up. Yet, his courage and optimism have fueled tremendous advances in medical research on paralysis and spinal injuries.

Michael J. Fox is another example of a man faced with a crippling disease channeling his courage and optimism into ridding the world of Parkinson's. Athletes in the Paralympics, wounded veterans, cancer survivors—these are all examples of folks who have summoned the courage to attack their misfortune with optimism, who have chosen to unleash their full potential. If you are particularly interested in this area, I'd highly recommend you read *The Adversity Advantage* by Paul G. Stoltz and Erik Weihenmayer (New York: Fireside, 2006).

Listen and Accept Reality Quickly

Many people think optimists are, by nature, idealists who rarely look at the world the way it really is. I respectfully disagree. I don't think that either optimism or pessimism is the primary behavior that defines how you look at the world. I think that honor goes to our ability (or lack of ability) to listen—really listen. Once we have really listened, we must also accept reality quickly.

Your optimism or pessimism will determine your actions, but before you act, you must first listen. We are generally lousy at this. It is one of our primary forms of communication, and yet we don't teach it in our schools. We have formal classes to teach kids to read, to write, to speak, but we don't have listening classes. And it shows. The vast majority of marriages fail because of our inability to listen and really understand what our partner is trying to communicate. Folks finally give up. How well do you listen to your husband, wife, girl-friend, boyfriend, son, daughter, brother, sister, teacher, coach, boss, direct reports, or peers?

And the issue isn't getting any easier with technology. Ironically, as if it weren't hard enough already, technology is now playing an ever-im-portant role in our listening. We have almost endless options to share what we're doing, where we are, and our opinions, but with so many devices at hand, it's actually getting harder to really listen. We're too busy checking email, checking the latest tweet or blog, texting, and so on. Active listening takes real courage today. And what takes just as much courage is, once you have listened, accepting reality quickly.

What does accepting reality quickly really mean? It means to take the action you know you should take. Don't postpone it. Don't ignore it. Don't sidestep it. As we were sailing across the world, we had to constantly listen to the signals we were getting from the sea, the sky, our single-sideband (long-range) radio, and one another. Not accepting reality quickly out at sea can be fatal. If the waves were building, the wind was building, and the sky looked green and stormy, we'd get ready for the storm. We'd reef the sails (make them smaller). We'd batten down all the hatches (secure them closed). We'd have some food ready just in case eating got difficult in the storm. We'd log our position and direction and would report it to someone via the radio if possible. We'd make sure the decks were clear of gear that could easily be turned into a missile at high wind speeds. We would check to see how each of us was feeling. You get the idea.

What we couldn't do is ignore the signals—not listen and not accept the reality that a storm was on its way. In the case of the big storm we experienced, that would undoubtedly have resulted in some sort of newspaper headline about a family lost at sea and feared dead!

Not many of you will physically sail across a stormy ocean, but metaphorically, this is happening every single day of your life. How well are you listening, and how much courage are you summoning up to accept reality quickly—and then acting to address it?

About fifteen years ago, the Crest team at P&G developed what they thought was an absolutely breakthrough idea. Most consumers really want to have whiter teeth—whiter than you can get from regular toothpaste. So the research and development team developed this new product innovation, which consisted of a clear strip with some whitener on it that you stick to your teeth a couple of times a day for a few weeks. The product's price was about $50. They tested the concept with consumers, and it bombed. I'm oversimplifying, but essentially the feedback they got was that no one used to paying $5 for a tube of Crest toothpaste could fathom paying $50 for this new innovation— even though they'd love to have much whiter teeth. Rather than kill the project, the team took the time to really listen and to accept reality quickly. They determined that the real challenge was not so much about the product. They needed to change the frame of reference for this new innovation away from toothpaste.

So they rewrote the concept—this time explaining that you could get the same whitening with $50 Crest Whitestrips that you could get from a $500 whitening treatment from your dentist. By really listening to consumers and by accepting the reality that the way they were presenting the idea was flawed, the team made the adjustments necessary for the innovation to resonate with consumers. In 2000, Crest Whitestrips launched an entirely new category. According to a report published by the American Academy of Cosmetic Dentistry, consumers now spend around $1.4 billion on teeth-whitening products annually,[16] and Crest commands a sixty-seven percent share of the whitestrips segment.[17]

If you are in business, how is your company really doing? How's the new product launch? *Too early to tell* is a familiar answer, but that's often

16   Diane Mapes, "Blindingly White," NBC News, updated January 17, 2007, http://www.nbcnews.com/id/15309784/ns/health-oral_health/t/ blindingly-white-teeth-bleaching-gone-too-far/#.Vurnnkugn19.

17   "P&G Wins Court Battle Over Crest 3D Whitestrips," *Cincinnati Business Courier*, September 23, 2014, http://www.bizjournals.com/cincinnati/news/2014/09/23/ p-g-wins-court-battle-over-crest-3d-whitestrips.html.

simply code for *Not as well as we'd like, but let's give it more time.* If you or your children are in college, how is school really going? Are you/ they so caught up in the day-to-day challenges of studying, getting good grades, and so on that you/they might forget to take a step back from time to time? Are you really where you want to be? Are you becoming the person you want to be? Are you studying what truly excites you? How are your relationships with your family? Friends? Colleagues?

Chances are high that you already know there are some storms of your own that are about to hit or that you're already in. Rather than ignoring them and letting them turn into full-fledged hurricanes, I strongly urge you to summon the courage to listen to what's going on around you and to have the courage to accept reality quickly. Then, whatever you choose to do, trust yourself and your team, and do it with optimism.

Get Your Hands Dirty

I think one of the most poorly designed systems on our sailboat was the toilet (known as a *head* on the boat). The mix of everything that passes through this system is called *blackwater*, but on land, it's more commonly known as *sewage*! The toilet itself works well most of the time. If you are within ten miles of shore, all blackwater must be held in a holding tank, which is then emptied out at an authorized pump-out station. This, of course, makes life a lot happier for all the sea creatures and humans who live along the waterfront or swim at the beach. If you are beyond ten miles of the shore, the blackwater is simply released directly into the open ocean.

The biggest problem with the system is the holding tank, which is notorious for clogging up at the little drainage tube. Our system on *Hakuna Matata* was no exception. Now you can well imagine that if this small tank gets blocked, it fills up pretty quickly, and it's not long before you have a very unhappy boat. The only practical way for me to fix the clogging issue was to hold my nose with one hand, open the top of the holding tank, reach down to the bottom of the tank, feel around the bottom, and stick my finger in the blocked hole and wiggle it around. Yep. Disgusting. But here's the lesson. The only way to fix the problem was to get my hands dirty! The great thing about this is that my efforts were instantly rewarded. The tank always emptied quickly, the stench went away, I'd wash my hands (thoroughly), and once again, we'd have a very happy crew.

This is a perfect analogy for each of our lives, both at home and at the office. Sometimes our holding tanks are clogged and are literally just filling up with crap. From time to time, our lives stink! There's this "regret" and that lost job and this failed relationship and that failed business project or venture.

If you let them, the people you trust can help you. But no one other than you is going to actually reach down into your holding tank and unclog it. There are some things you just can't delegate! This is something you have to do, and only you can do it. Similar to what I did on the boat, the minute you reach your hand into the muck and clear it out, you are rewarded instantly. You can literally feel the tank emptying of all that baggage. It's very liberating and actually gives you the space in your life to focus on the present and the future and to realize the dreams in your LifeBoat instead of being weighed down by the past.

The same applies to companies. Most companies are desperate for innovation to accelerate sales and stay ahead of the competition. Yet, their holding tanks are filled with crap that won't allow it to happen: too much bureaucracy, action that is too slow, fear of failure, poor strategy, egotistical leaders, or a lack of consumer understanding. Your job as a leader—of people, of processes, or of a project—is to have the courage to get your hands dirty, to address the real issues that are clogging up your holding tank, reach down, wiggle your finger—and fix it!

In my career, I had one boss who was a shining example of not being afraid to get his hands dirty. He discovered that in one of our factories several corrupt leaders were taking bribes and breaking the law. He decided that he needed to make an example of them, not only to demonstrate that their behavior was unacceptable but also to make it very clear to everyone across the entire organization that this kind of behavior would not be tolerated. He marched into the factory along with the police. He had the leaders arrested and led out in handcuffs in front of everyone. Folks at the company still talk about the incident to this day.

Have Fun

As you reflect on your circle of family, friends, and colleagues, who do you like to spend time with? Is it the whiner for whom nothing ever goes right and who is always miserable? The traffic is against him or her, and so is the weather, the boss, "them," and "the system." For most people, the answer is a pretty emphatic no.

We all have our quirks and idiosyncrasies, so it's obviously fine to have friends who are a challenge every once in a while. I am not suggesting for a minute that you abandon family, friends, or colleagues in their time of need! But it's really hard to be around someone who never has any fun! Even when we are faced with challenges and problems, you'll come out better on the other side if you summon the courage to have fun, or develop this ability if you don't already have it.

Kids know how to do this. There is a widespread urban myth that children laugh between three hundred and five hundred times a day, while adults only laugh about fifteen to twenty. Irrespective of the number, if we don't laugh—we're missing out on all the health benefits.

Laughter helps us physically be able to achieve our dreams. According to the Mayo Clinic, laughter not only reduces the levels of stress hormones (cortisol, epinephrine, dopamine) in our bodies, but it actually increases the level of health-enhancing hormones, known as endorphins. It increases the production of antibodies in our bodies and enhances T cells, which together strengthen our immune system.[18] Wow!

As senior vice president of the Global Snacks group for PepsiCo, a big part of my job was to get all the countries around the world excited about the company's strategies and to inspire them to use those strategies to frame their local plans. But I also needed to deepen their understanding of the business we had around the world for us to be as effective as possible as a team. So rather than always hold global meetings at the company's headquarters in Purchase, New York, I made them a lot more fun. I'd schedule the meetings in different countries, and instead of just sitting in meeting rooms all day for three days straight, we would always dedicate a day to cultural immersion.

The team ventured out in a bus through India's countryside to visit the Taj Mahal, experiencing all the chaos, color, and fun that is India along the way. We explored the ancient sacred city of Teotihuacan just thirty miles northeast of Mexico City. We explored all the monuments, sites, and pubs around London. We explored the great Sagrada Familia Basilica in Barcelona, and the tango clubs of Argentina. Rather than view our global meetings as bureaucratic obligations, the team looked forward to them. They were fully engaged and had fun. Their knowledge expanded, and their teamwork deepened—and I am convinced it is one of the key reasons why our business growth accelerated.

———————————

18   Mayo Clinic Staff, "Stress Relief from Laughter? It's No Joke," *Healthy Lifestyle* newsletter, July 23, 2013, http://www.mayoclinic.org/healthy-lifestyle/stress-management/in-depth/stress-relief/art-20044456.

Not many folks get to explore the world like that—but there are literally millions of ways to inject fun into work. One of my neighbors who works at the local sports shop brings donuts and coffee in for his team every Friday. It's a fun weekly ritual that everyone looks forward to and that deepens the team's connections. Other neighbors who own a lawn-care franchise take their team go-carting. Google has ping-pong tables and video games for their associates to play and "let off steam."

On *Hakuna Matata*, dolphins would often join us mid-ocean, doing flips and squealing in delight. They know how to have fun—and it was contagious. We'd have smiles on our faces for days. Just because this whole adventure called life and work is serious stuff—don't forget to summon the courage to have fun along the way. You'll be happier, and your results (however you define them) will be better.

Create Shared Dreams

Perhaps the most important adventure on my list of dreams was starting a family, and I was making no progress whatsoever early on. As a young man in my twenties, I had a nasty habit of running away from relationships. I had this vague dream of finding someone I wanted to spend the rest of my life with, but after dating someone for a while, I'd get scared and run away, thinking I'd have to sacrifice all my dreams in the process of making a commitment.

Again, I was faced with a binary *choice*: Either change the dream or change the behavior. My wife and I laugh that this is $10,000 worth of therapy talking (it's not really). I decided to change my behavior and was helped along in a big way when my girlfriend at the time simply declared to me directly one day that she didn't want to make my dreams smaller; she just wanted to make them bigger. I was still a bit slow on the uptake (as she will attest), but over time, I made the choice to change my behavior and didn't run away!

I proposed to Pat in Barcelona. We were married in Los Angeles in 1993. After a honeymoon in Costa Rica, Pat joined me to live in a rooftop apartment in Stockholm. She had given up her job, sold her house, sold her car, gotten married, and moved out of the country—all within the space of two weeks. How lucky was I? She has remained completely true to her commitment of filling up our LifeBoat, making our dreams bigger, and I couldn't be more blessed to have her as my wife and the mother of our kids.

I'll admit that sometimes I drive her a bit crazy ("What do you want to do next . . . climb Everest?"), but we still sit down together every so often to review our dreams and check in with each other on the big stuff. Our dreams have evolved, and as is often the case, many are now wrapped up in the dreams we have for our kids to be happy, healthy, and fulfilled adults. But midway through this adventure called life—we still plan to be as intentional as we possibly can be about our dreams.

• • •

Courage, therefore, is not an option. It's a necessity. As I said at the outset of this chapter, it is the catalyst that enables you to bring the dreams in your LifeBoat to life—both in business and in all the aspects of your personal life. It enables you to declare those dreams to the world and to be so intentional that you have everyone talking about them. It is the catalyst that gives you the stamina to plan and prepare well. As such, it helps you ignite your dreams and make them happen. It is not one simple concept. As I have illustrated here, courage has many layers and is complex. You will need to summon courage in multiple areas, depending on where you are in your life and what obstacles you need to overcome.

Take the time to reflect not only on what this means for you but also on how you can go about building your courage and resolve to make your most important dreams happen. As I have noted throughout this chapter, like most things in life that you want to be good at, courage typically takes practice. The more you practice it, the more courageous you will become. Ski jumpers don't suddenly summon the courage to jump off an Olympic-sized ski jump. They work up to it, starting small, and then becoming more courageous as their skills increase. You don't just summon up the courage to sail around the world. You build the skills, one little courageous step at a time, until you are finally ready to go. You don't build a business empire overnight. It typically takes small acts of courage, which get bigger and bigger over time, as your confidence and skill increase.

CHART YOUR COURSE

I'd recommend a similar approach with the LifeBoat list you have made in the back of the book. Let's jump back to page 156. What are the small steps of courage that you can begin to implement starting tomorrow to practice building your courage and to increase your level of comfort with it? I've included a list of prompts and challenges to incite you to action, so that the dreams you have already written down (and the ones you haven't yet written down) can really come to life.

CHAPTER 6

Launch Your LifeBoat!

Everything starts with a dream. So we all have a LifeBoat full of dreams. We have dreams for all the aspects of our personal lives, and dreams for our careers and work lives. Whatever they are, they tend to be deeply personal and also tend to get us fired up. Yet, far too many go unrealized. How frustrating that the vast majority of us and the vast majority of businesses will die full of potential. As the American poet Eugene F. Ware once said, "All glory comes from daring to begin!" You've just got to call all dreams on deck and launch your LifeBoat because there's no time to lose.

An important lesson regarding our dream to sail the world is that it took a long time for the dream to take shape and happen. Shortly after we were married, Pat and I sat down and did the LifeBoat exercise together. (I've laid out a worksheet at the back of the book to help you with this exercise. It basically means she wrote down a list of all her dreams, I wrote down a list of all my dreams, we prioritized our own lists, then got together to talk through them with each other.) Pat's list was long, and so was mine. After all, we had an exciting, yet undefined, future ahead of us. Sailing the world was high on my priority list, and traveling the world was high on Pat's, so we merged them into one dream for our lives together. That was probably around 1995.

Getting specific, I mean really specific, about the dream took years. Getting intentional about bringing it to life took a long time too—and it wasn't without its share of setbacks. When we kept our eyes squarely focused on the dream, we were high up on the ladder of intentionality. When we took our eyes off the ball, our intentionality often dipped. The planning and preparation was extensive and took years. It wasn't until 2005 that I sat down with PepsiCo to talk everything through, and get Pedro's, Mike's, and Steve's support for the plan. And it wasn't until 2006 that construction of *Hakuna Matata* began in South Africa at the boatyard of Robertson and Caine.

Then in 2007, twelve years after we hatched the plan, we actually took the kids out of school and set sail on an amazing family adventure that took us throughout the Mediterranean, down the northwest coast of Africa, across the Atlantic, throughout the Caribbean, through the Panama Canal, to the Galapagos Islands, across the Pacific, through the islands of the South Pacific, to Australia. **We did it.**

The dream of living and working internationally also took time to materialize. The first time I articulated this dream to my management team at P&G was in 1987, a year after I joined the company. I needed to prove to them that I was a strong performer, that I could really add value to subsidiaries outside the United States, and that I could adapt and thrive in different settings. It wasn't until 1991 that I was actually posted to the company's Stockholm office.

Michael Phelps's dream of becoming an Olympic champion took years to realize. JFK's dream for the United States to send a man safely to the moon and back took the best part of a decade. Martin Luther King Jr.'s dream of racial equality in the United States has still not been fully realized, but there are still people working every day to make it happen.

What I am underscoring here is that often—especially with the big dreams—they take time and endurance to make happen. There's rarely a "quick fix." You might find it rather disheartening after having read this book if you think you have to wait five to ten years to see the results! Honestly, for some dreams that will be the case, but it won't be for most of them—because not all your dreams are huge. Sure, the majority of the examples and dreams that I've discussed have tended toward the bigger end of the scale: homeownership, running a company, living in different countries all over the world, finding a life partner, and sailing around the world. I've mostly used these big examples to really drive home the point of each section.

If your takeaway is that my suggestions are therefore limited only to the big adventures—then I've failed to get my message across. Life is fueled by achieving both the big dreams and the smaller dreams along the way—and there is absolutely no reason why this can't apply to everything you'd like to achieve in your life, no matter how big or small. Assuming you can articulate your big dreams specifically, and have them driving the overall direction of your company, your projects, your life—then you can easily follow the same approach with your small dreams.

What are some of your smaller, but equally important, dreams? Achieving a certain level of fitness? Visiting your parents more often? Reading more? Getting the business review done on time? Improving your skills or performance at a sport? Becoming a better leader? Getting your partner to share in the housework? Taking that vacation to a spot you've always dreamed of? Buying that car? Saving for this or that? Learning how to play an instrument? Getting your kid back on track with his or her studies? I am obviously not going to list all the possibilities because the book would never end—but if you reframe all of these as specific dreams, and adopt this approach, you are going to realize many more than you are realizing today and will be well on your way to unleashing your full potential, as defined by you.

At this point, you may well be thinking, "This is all well and good, but I don't know which questions to ask, or what to do next." You've just got to launch your LifeBoat! Let's take a relatively big example and run it from beginning to end. One of the key engines of growth for any economy is business start-ups. There are literally hundreds of thousands of people in the United States who have either started their own business or dreamed of starting their own business. Some of these people have radically reshaped the world we live in, and yet they all started small. If I reflect on many of the major industries and employers today, a huge percentage didn't even exist when I was in college— the personal computer industry, the Internet, cell phones, and social media, just to name a few. So let's say you have a dream of starting your business. Here we go.

Starting Your Own Business

Clearly it's not enough to want to start your own business. The first thing you need to do is define what business you want to be in and why. Just jumping into a business because you think it will make you rich is typically a bad idea. As mentioned earlier, the failure rate in businesses is usually in the ninety-plus percent range—so jumping on some bandwagon in hopes of quick money rarely works out. If you are old enough to remember the Internet boom and subsequent bust—you'll recall that a lot of people started businesses to make a quick buck and get out. That was their primary motive, and most of them failed. Making money or lots of money is typically the result of doing something really well. It is a consequence. The successes are generally individuals and companies

that have identified an unmet need in any given market (whether articulated or not) and that have created a superior product or service to
meet that need.

DREAM SPECIFICALLY!

To start getting specific about your dream, ask yourself what you are
passionate about and what you would be prepared to dedicate your life
to. What do you believe so strongly in that you are prepared to take some
risk? What products, or services, are you interested in starting? What
are the unmet needs in that market/category? What are the barriers to
usage or barriers to purchase and consumption? What are the problems/
issues with existing products/services that have not been addressed?
What does the market look like? Who is the competition? How are they
doing? What are their sources of competitive advantage? What is your
core idea? Is it highly distinctive? Is it highly relevant? Is it both?

As mentioned earlier, if your company, product, or service is highly
distinctive but not relevant, then in all likelihood it will be a fad. It will
come and go. If you build a business model that anticipates that—you
can be very successful. You get in, create or fuel the fad, ride the wave,
and get out when it's no longer hot. In this scenario, you would not
invest in building a big company infrastructure, because you need to get
in and out within a few years.

Alternatively, if your business, product, or service is highly relevant and not distinctive, it will likely be a commodity. Think about the
regular lightbulb. How many of us go into the store with a particular
brand of lightbulb in mind? (Very few.) For a product or service to be
successful in the commodity space, you typically need to be the low-
cost producer—because you won't be able to price your product at
a premium. Margins will be low, and you will need to generate high
volume to make money.

Where I'd strongly suggest you want to land—is on a product or service that is highly relevant **and** highly distinctive. Think of the businesses, brands, and services that are part of your everyday life. Chances are, for you, they are both relevant and distinctive, and this is where you want your company or service to be. If you are both relevant and distinctive, you are well on the way to developing a strong, sustainable business.

There is a terrific book by Marty Neumeier entitled *ZAG: The Number-One Strategy of High-Performance Brands* (Berkeley, CA: New Riders, 2007). In it, he shares a very simple, yet powerful, tool—your "onliness" statement—where he challenges readers to clearly define how they are the **only** product or service that does "this particular thing" for "these particular consumers/customers" in "this particular geography" in "this particular era." It forces you to get specific. If you can't articulate your onliness statement clearly and succinctly, do as Marty suggests—keep going back to it until you can; otherwise, you will likely end up being a "me too" in the market and reduce your probability of success. This concept will help you get specific about your dream.

I am in the process of a new adventure—launching a new snack company called The United Snacks of America with some partners of mine. One of our new brands is called Farmer's Pantry. Here's our onliness statement: "Farmer's Pantry is the **only** snack that combines meat and vegetables into a hearty, crunchy, wholesome snack for everyday Americans aged twenty to thirty to satisfy their hunger throughout the day in an era when the three-meal-a-day routine is breaking down." We are very specific about what it is, the category in which it competes, who it is for, and when it is to be consumed.

Once you've decided what your business is going to be, and how you are going to be distinctive, relevant, and unique, you must start making it time bound. When are you going to launch? Our target launch date is four months from the writing of this chapter. That's not much time—and it will require a high degree of intentionality from the team, outstanding planning and preparation, and a high degree of courage from us all.

CLIMB THE LADDER OF INTENTIONALITY!

Are you just thinking about starting this business, or are you so intentional that you have not only written it down and declared it—but you also have others talking about it? Assuming you are passionate about your idea and you are able to clearly articulate your specific dream—I suggest you start telling all your family and friends about it. Fire them up! You don't have all the details yet—but you are committed to making it happen. You're so excited about this new adventure that you can't stop thinking and talking about it. Here's what we're telling our friends and family:

> We are going to launch this exciting new business called Farmer's Pantry four months from now into grocery stores and convenience stores across the country! It will be the first snack in the market that combines meats and vegetables into a convenient, hearty, crunchy snack for everyday Americans to satisfy their hunger—a 'crossover snack' that combines the best of meals and the best of snacks. We're only going to source ingredients from American family farms. The ingredients will all be authentic ingredients that you can identify and that you'd find in a farmer's pantry. Another really cool part of this is that we are going to give back to American family farms—to help them thrive, not just survive.

Contrast this with:

> I'm working on a new snack idea with some friends, and
> we're hoping that we are going to be able to launch it
> sometime soon.

That second declaration gives the illusion of intentionality—but it
is not intentional at all. As Yoda once said in *Star Wars: The Empire Strikes
Back*, "Do. Or do not. There is no try."

PLAN AND PREPARE AS THOUGH YOUR DREAMS
DEPEND ON IT—BECAUSE THEY DO!

The business you're going to start will be specific to you. You may be
able to start big, or you may want to start small. You may be your own
investor, or maybe the family is going to lend you money. Whoever is
supporting you—keep them in the loop about how you are planning
and preparing for your business to be a success. The more you do this—
the more confidence you will build. You will build your confidence in
your idea. You will build their confidence that your idea is real. It will
keep them engaged and enthusiastic—and it will force you to be better.

With the specific dream for Farmer's Pantry, and a high degree of
intentionality around when and where we are going to launch the business, we have to make sure that we are doing everything we possibly can
to increase our chances of success. We have to plan and prepare well.

We started our planning by examining the market to identify an
important and relevant unmet consumer need. From this, we know
that a lot of people are eating less of the "three meals a day"—and are
"grazing" throughout the day to satisfy their hunger. As a result, there
is a trend that I call the "snackification of meals." There is a trend where
consumers are placing increased importance on the ability to identify
the authentic ingredients in their food (not the case with many snacks).

When you add this and several other trends together, it is clear that many folks in the United States are on the go and hungry for a convenient, hearty, crunchy, wholesome snack that's made with authentic ingredients from American farms. We have linked data, insights, and knowledge to define this opportunity. We have tested the idea with consumers across the country to see whether they find it to be both distinctive and relevant—and they do.

Convinced that we have a big idea, we summoned the courage to find some investors, and pitched them the idea. They decided to fund the development of the proposition and product—so not only did we set sail, but also we started to really venture out into the unknown. We spent time with a research and development company to develop a lineup of superior products to meet the unmet need. We tested the first round with consumers, and it didn't go so well. We learned a lot about what was working with the product, and what was not. We sat down with some retailers and brokers to solicit their input. Having really listened and accepted reality quickly (that the product still needed work)—we went back to our research and development partners and reworked the product until we felt like we had a winner.

We asked ourselves many questions that enabled us to plan and prepare a robust marketing plan, a high-quality manufacturing plan, an efficient and effective distribution plan, and of course a powerful sales plan. We shared all this with our investors on a weekly basis to build their intentionality and enthusiasm for the new business. We are well on our way—but a mountain of work still needs to happen to make all the ideas that we put down on paper for this business adventure really come to life.

BE COURAGEOUS!

There is a famous saying that "All glory comes from daring to begin." At some point, you will have done all the planning and preparing you can for your new business. Now you have to summon the courage you need to actually get it started—recognizing that even with all your preparation, it may still not work out.

Because we have so much belief in our specific dream for this business, and we are so intentional about making it happen, it has enabled us to really build our courage and confidence to forge ahead.

In 2015, we took our Farmer's Pantry brand proposition and our handmade samples and launched it at one of the biggest trade shows in the country—the National Association of Convenience Stores show in Las Vegas. We had a small booth. We made Farmer's Pantry display materials, shirts and caps, high-quality samples of our products and our packaging, business cards, sell sheets, a website, and a price sheet. We looked like a real company. We sold the brand hard to anyone who would give us the time. Almost everybody was excited about the idea, loved the branding and the package design, and loved the product. We came away with a list of over sixty important buyers across the country—who are interested in buying Farmer's Pantry to put in their hundreds of thousands of stores. Not only did we have the courage to set sail, we also had the courage to venture out into the unknown.

As we look ahead, we now have to summon the courage to get everything in place to bring this new company to life in the next four months. We have to have the courage to keep going in the face of adversity (which we will no doubt encounter). We have to have the courage to be humble so that we can learn and adapt to the needs of the market. We have to have the courage to ask for help—from our suppliers and from each other—and give it. We have to have the courage to trust each other and ourselves; the courage to listen, and accept reality quickly; and the courage to have fun while doing it.

The story of whether Farmer's Pantry is successful or not has yet to be written. Our dream, of course, is that it will be and that we will have done everything we possibly can to make it happen. But it could fail, and the statistics would suggest it's likely to. That's the risk we take in putting in all the time, effort, and money to launch this business. But we can't let that fear paralyze us—otherwise it will prevent us from ever unleashing our full potential. We simply have to adopt Thomas Edison's famous mind-set—"Failure is the opportunity to begin again more intelligently!"—and begin again. My discussion of Farmer's Pantry is a high-level, oversimplified example of putting all the steps we've covered to work. It is designed simply to step you through how to approach the dreams in your LifeBoat—whether they are big or small.

Whatever your dreams, and wherever they may take you, one of my dreams is that this book, in some way, helps you get your dreams back if you've lost them; realize them if you're a bit stuck in the mud; identify dreams if you don't have any right now; and truly unleash your full potential. There is no certainty; there is only adventure—so go for it. All Dreams on Deck!

CHART YOUR COURSE

With this perspective, go to page 161, and put everything together in your Captain's Log. You have identified your Grab Bags—the most important elements of your LifeBoat. You have articulated the dreams for each Grab Bag with specificity and prioritized your most important dreams. You have identified some key steps to climb up the ladder of intentionality for those dreams, and you have identified some key actions to take in order not only to plan and prepare well but also to build your courage. In short, you have charted the course for your life and work. The Captain's Log is simply a tool to energize you and for you to use to hold yourself accountable for unleashing your full potential—as defined by you.

The Chart Plotter

You are the captain of your own LifeBoat! So think of this section of the book as your "chart plotter." A chart plotter is a sailing instrument used to chart your course and keep you on track. By using this workbook, you are literally plotting the course for your dreams. Each section is linked to a chapter in the book, and is specifically designed to enable you to create a tangible plan and take action. The first few exercises are designed to help you define where you want to go in your life and work. The subsequent exercises are designed to help you plot the course to get there. As is always the case, the more effort you put into it, the more useful it will be. Have fun—it's time to get all your dreams on deck!

Waypoints are specific points on the Earth's surface. They are typically given as coordinates that reflect latitude and longitude. In sailing, waypoints are often used to *build a route to a specific destination*. We will use the same term throughout the development of your Chart Plotter as each waypoint is an important step in charting your course.

AHOY! is a commonly used sailing term, and it is used to draw your attention to something. You'll find the use of the term whenever I want to point out something specific for you to think about or act upon.

CHARTING YOUR COURSE

The Most Important Elements of Your Life

Your **LifeBoat** is critically important. It keeps you afloat on the sea of life and it's the vessel that will carry you to discovering your dreams.

Before you set out to chart the course for your life and work, take some time now to make a list of all the important elements in your life. These are all of the unique, individual events, activities, and hobbies that take up your time and brainpower. What are the most important components of your life? Family, Friends, Work, Faith, Fitness, Finances, Spirit?

A. Husband
B. Kids
C. Large Family
D. Security
E. Health Costs & Family
F. — physical health
G. — emotional health

H. Environment
I. Learning
J. Faith
K. Using my gifts to help others
L.
M.
N.

Of the elements listed above, pick and circle the 6–8 most important ones to include in your LifeBoat. These are the *most important components* of your life that you feel define you as a person (work, social, etc.). They are your **Grab Bags**, the elements of your life that are most important to your LifeBoat.

>>> AHOY!

Now, without overthinking this, assign a score to each Grab Bag in order to determine how full or 'healthy' it is. A score of 1 means the Grab Bag is empty or in full crisis. A score of 10 means full to the brim or phenomenal. This will be helpful as you define which areas to focus on first.

CHARTING YOUR COURSE

Dream Like You Mean It

DREAMS: ROUND 1

Before you chart the course for your life and work, you need to determine the destinations. Set a timer for at least fifteen minutes and list as many dreams you have—both big and small—in the order that they come to you. What is important in this first pass is *quantity, not quality*. Step away from the list a couple of times (get a coffee or something stronger!), then come back to it and *keep adding*. You likely have many more dreams than you realize at first. We just don't often take the time to really think about them, or write them all down.

---------------------------------   ---------------------------------
---------------------------------   ---------------------------------
---------------------------------   ---------------------------------
---------------------------------   ---------------------------------
---------------------------------   ---------------------------------
---------------------------------   ---------------------------------
---------------------------------   ---------------------------------
---------------------------------   ---------------------------------
---------------------------------   ---------------------------------
---------------------------------   ---------------------------------
---------------------------------   ---------------------------------
---------------------------------   ---------------------------------
---------------------------------   ---------------------------------

DREAMS: ROUND 2

Now that you've got a list of your dreams, we'll need to fit each one into a Grab Bag for your LifeBoat. Refer back to the previous list, and assign your dreams to one of your Grab Bags. If you have similar items, it's ok to group them as one dream. (Use the blank space below and in the subsequent sections to scribble down any relevant notes.)

>>> **AHOY!**

You may want to ask your spouse or partner to complete this list, too, and then compare your results. This will help you understand which dreams you have in common and can help you each realize more of your personal dreams in the long run. I guarantee you'll learn something new about each other in the process, no matter how long you have been together.

DREAMS: ROUND 3

Look at the lists of dreams that you compiled in the previous activity. Now pick out and circle the five most important dreams on your list. *Note: If two dreams seem similar, try to think of a way to combine them into one more detailed dream.*

››› AHOY!

Where do you stand relative to each of these important dreams? On-track? Really? Off track? Try to give yourself as honest an appraisal as possible. Again, you may find it helpful to use a scale. 1 is completely off track, 10 is couldn't be more on track.

DREAMS: ROUND 4

Now it's time to get specific about your most important dreams! Write down more details about each of these five dreams. Think about what each dream means to you, why you want to accomplish it, and how accomplishing it might impact your life. By when do you want to have achieved the dream? What *specifically* do you want for that dream, and by when? If finances play a role in the dream, how much money will you need? What are the other details you need to consider? In short, get as specific as possible!

››› **AHOY!**

Be sure that your answers are specific to your personal dreams. If your dream is to start your own business, what type of business do you want to start? If your dream is to retire early, how much money do you actually need in your savings account to fund a comfortable retirement? If your dream is to buy your own home, consider what size home you would like and where you would like it to be.

Dream 1:

_____

_____

_____

_____

Dream 2:

_____

_____

_____

_____

Dream 3:

_____

_____

_____

_____

Dream 4:

_____

_____

_____

_____

Dream 5:

_____

_____

_____

_____

Climb Your Ladder of Intentionality

At this point, you have summoned all your dreams on deck. Congratulations! You have defined the destinations for the dreams in each of your Grab Bags with clarity and specificity. With this clarity you can now begin charting the course for your life and work. It starts with intentionality.

WAYPOINT #1

Define where are you on the ladder of intentionality for each of these dreams, with 1 meaning really low intentionality and 10 meaning highly intentional.

Write down some of the actions you can take tomorrow to climb up the ladder of intentionality. Tell a family member/someone you love? Tell friend or colleague you trust? Declare your most important dreams more broadly or with more specifics? Make a list of people to share each of your dreams with and define when you'll do it. Consider what you will say to each of these people at that time. After you finish the list, sit down with your spouse or another loved one and tell them about your dreams. You may get some pushback and questions, but they will be coming from a place of support. The more you declare your dreams, the more intentional you will become. Don't focus on all the things that could go wrong or get in the way. Focus on inspiring yourself and those around you.

DREAM 1 {#dream-1} SCORE

STEP

WHEN

NOTES

DREAM 2 SCORE

STEP

WHEN

NOTES

DREAM 3 SCORE

STEP

WHEN

NOTES

DREAM 4 SCORE

STEP

WHEN

NOTES

DREAM 5 SCORE

STEP

WHEN

NOTES

CHARTING YOUR COURSE

Ready Yourself, Your Crew, and Your Ship

WAYPOINT #2

Answer the following questions about each of your dreams. Be as specific, detailed, and honest as you possibly can.

Need more specificity in dreams. Like "Camino" journey.

Need routine (day & week).

››› AHOY!

How well are you planning and preparing for each of your most important dreams to be realized? Be sure to assess yourself honestly. If you're like most people, there is more that you can be doing to visualize, plan for, and realize your dreams. Take this opportunity to look back on your notes for this chapter and see if there's anything else you can add.

Dream 1: *Katherine, move on to lead a happy, content and independent life. At peace, fulfilling social relationships*

1. Overall, what does planning and preparation look like for this dream? *Really get detailed on this! Be as descriptive as you can!*

2. What do I need to know, do, and know how to do to accomplish this?

   Big ?.

3. What equipment do I need?

   Therapist for me/us/ Kath. Strong healthy & positive relationship w/ Kath. Time & effort to do what is best for her. Strength, toughness, candor.

4. Will I need help from other people? If so, who? What will I need? When will I need it?

   Our therapist; Katherine's team (therapist, psychiatrist, group work). ASAP

Dream 2: _Deeper & more Sulfilling relationship with RJ._

1. Overall, what does planning and preparation look like for this dream? *Really get detailed on this! Be as descriptive as you can!*

   Make the committment. All in, not put myself & wants above it.

2. What do I need to know, do, and know how to do to accomplish this?

   Committment, patientience, unselfishness.

   Effort from him. Calmness, slowdown
   ↳ Goal we share can work towards together.

3. What equipment do I need?

   Shotgun, patience. Exucise first thing in morning. 6:30am wake up schedule

4. Will I need help from other people? If so, who? What will I need? When will I need it?

Dream 3: _Work to be as healthy physically as we can (RJ & myself)._

1. Overall, what does planning and preparation look like for this dream? *Really get detailed on this! Be as descriptive as you can!*

Find doctor; physical exam great.

Dentist, Dr, OBGYN

2. What do I need to know, do, and know how to do to accomplish this?

Discipline, exercise schedule. Cooking & food plan; reduce alcohol consumption.

3. What equipment do I need?

4. Will I need help from other people? If so, who? What will I need? When will I need it?

Dream 4: _Contribute, give back to world. Make a difference._

1. Overall, what does planning and preparation look like for this dream? *Really get detailed on this! Be as descriptive as you can!*

   → may need to learn Spanish?
   → daily schedule so have work time
   → Time exploring options

2. What do I need to know, do, and know how to do to accomplish this?

   Exposure, thought as to what direction / directions to Take

3. What equipment do I need?

   → Computer skills / better technology

4. Will I need help from other people? If so, who? What will I need? When will I need it?

   yes.

Dream 5: _Reconnect w/ God and strengthen my faith._

1. Overall, what does planning and preparation look like for this dream? *Really get detailed on this! Be as descriptive as you can!*

   _____

   _____

   _____

   _____

   _____

2. What do I need to know, do, and know how to do to accomplish this?

   Step out & get involved w/ Christ Church.

   Schedule 1 a day / week.

   _____

   _____

3. What equipment do I need?

   _____

   _____

   _____

   _____

   _____

4. Will I need help from other people? If so, who? What will I need? When will I need it?

   Yes

   _____

   _____

   _____

   _____

CHARTING YOUR COURSE

Summon Your Courage

WAYPOINT #3A

Courage isn't something that we get good at overnight. Courage is a muscle that we build over time by practicing being more courageous. Take a few minutes to brainstorm ways that you can start building your courage muscles and increasing your comfort level with going after your dreams.

Here are a few challenges to get you started:

- What is the scariest part of planning your dream? What are you most afraid of, should you succeed or should you fail?

- Make a plan to implement some of the scariest aspects of your dream.

- What are some little things you can do every day to overcome your fear and gradually stretch your courage muscle?

- What are you passionate about and what are you prepared to dedicate your life to?

- What do you believe in so strongly that you're willing to take some risk?

WAYPOINT #3B

Now that you've taken a few minutes to brainstorm, it's time to really figure out how you can build the courage to accomplish your dreams. And don't get scared. Remember—the more you practice, the more comfortable you will get, and the more courageous you'll become. Jot down how you can be more courageous about your dreams below.

Dream 1:

_____

_____

_____

_____

_____

Dream 2:

_____

_____

_____

_____

_____

Dream 3:

_____

_____

_____

_____

_____

Dream 4:

_____

_____

_____

_____

_____

_____

Dream 5:

_____

_____

_____

_____

_____

_____

››› AHOY!

How courageous are you relative to each of the most important dreams in each Grab Bag? Be honest! No matter where you are now, you can and will improve. Honesty now will help you know where to start growing. Look back over the list you've just made. Which actions are you most excited about? Which actions scare you the most? If none of them scare you, go back and come up with something that will challenge you a little more!

Captain's Log

Congratulations. You have identified your Grab Bags; prioritized your most important dreams; articulated those dreams with specificity; and charted your course to climb up the ladder of intentionality, plan and prepare well, and summon your courage. On the next several pages, put all of these steps together for your most important dreams. This is your Captain's Log. It should not only inspire you but should also hold you accountable for unleashing your full potential. Refer to it often, and you will be well on your way not only to calling all dreams on deck but to actually making them happen.

››› **AHOY!**

Go back throughout all of the Charting Your Course steps of this section and compare you answers with your spouse's. Compare your long-term and short-term goals, and think of ways you can help each other achieve them.

DREAM 1:

_____
_____
_____
_____
_____
_____
_____
_____
_____
_____

THIS WEEK I WILL . . .

GOAL	DATE

THIS MONTH I WILL . . .

GOAL	DATE

THIS YEAR I WILL . . .

GOAL	DATE

DREAM 2:

_____

_____

_____

_____

_____

_____

_____

_____

_____

_____

THIS WEEK I WILL . . .

GOAL	DATE

THIS MONTH I WILL . . .

GOAL	DATE

THIS YEAR I WILL . . .

GOAL	DATE

DREAM 3:

_____

_____

_____

_____

_____

_____

_____

_____

_____

THIS WEEK I WILL . . .

GOAL	DATE

THIS MONTH I WILL . . .

GOAL	DATE

THIS YEAR I WILL . . .

GOAL	DATE

DREAM 4:

_____

_____

_____

_____

_____

_____

_____

_____

_____

_____

THIS WEEK I WILL . . .

GOAL	DATE

THIS MONTH I WILL . . .

GOAL	DATE

THIS YEAR I WILL . . .

GOAL	DATE

DREAM 5:

_____

_____

_____

_____

_____

_____

_____

_____

_____

_____

THIS WEEK I WILL . . .

GOAL	DATE

THIS MONTH I WILL . . .

GOAL	DATE

THIS YEAR I WILL . . .

GOAL	DATE

About the Author

Jeremy Cage's life mission is to help unleash the full potential of as many businesses and as many people as he possibly can. His business experience spans three decades of delivering strong, profitable business growth for Procter & Gamble, Schering-Plough Healthcare, PepsiCo, The Lighting Science Group, and his own firm, The Cage Group. He is a truly global citizen, having lived and worked in Germany, France, Belgium, Sweden, the United Kingdom, Venezuela, Brazil, Mexico, and the United States.

Jeremy believes that most businesses and most people—regardless of how successful they have been to date—do not actually achieve their full potential *as defined by them*. Committed to not letting that happen in his own life, he embarked on a sixteen-month voyage to sail the world, with his wife, Pat, and their kids, Bradley and Elena. This stretched his leadership skills, built his courage, pushed him beyond his comfort zone, and stimulated his creativity through interactions with new cultures and people.

Through business and life adventures, Jeremy's unique experience forms the foundation of the tools he uses to create breakthrough strategy, marketing, innovation, and people solutions for a diverse range of Fortune 500 companies.

Mercy Way by Fitzroy
Tues 7pm Beeches library - Florida last Tues.
        Domino Essect   authors

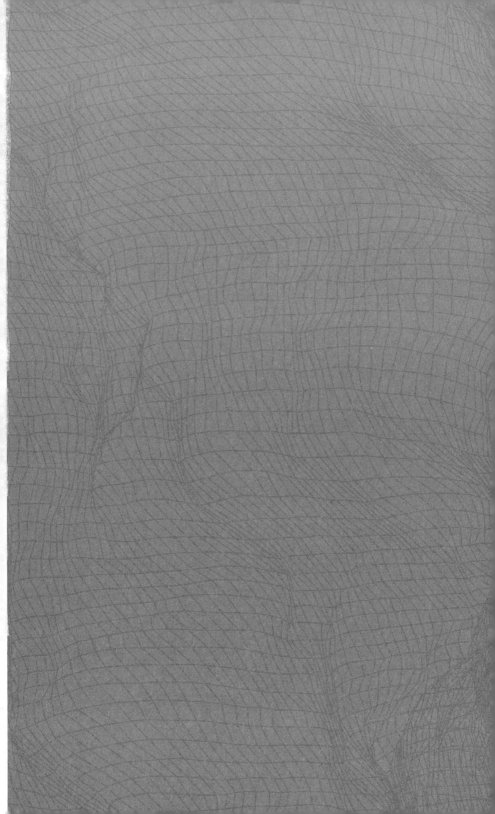